On Spiritual Strivings

SUNY series in Women in Education
Margaret Grogan, editor

On Spiritual Strivings

Transforming an African American Woman's Academic Life

CYNTHIA B. DILLARD

STATE UNIVERSITY OF NEW YORK PRESS

Cover photo taken by the author

Published by
State University of New York Press, Albany

© 2006 State University of New York

All rights reserved

Printed in the United States of America

For information, address State University of New York Press
194 Washington Avenue, Suite 305, Albany, NY 12210-2384

Production by Judith Block
Marketing by Anne M. Valentine

Library of Congress Cataloging-in-Publication Data

Dillard, Cynthia B., 1957–
  On spiritual strivings : transforming an African American woman's academic life /
Cynthia B. Dillard.
      p. cm. — (SUNY series in women in education)
  Includes bibliographical references and index.
  ISBN 0-7914-6811-9 (hardcover : alk. paper)
  1. African American women—Education (Higher) 2. Feminism and education—
United States. 3. Discrimination in higher education—United States. I. Title.
II. Series.

LC2781.D48 2006
378.1'.9822—dc22

2005026770

ISBN-13: 978-0-7914-6811-1 (hardcover: alk. paper)

10 9 8 7 6 5 4 3 2 1

In memory of my father-teachers
on both sides of the water,
Clyde Dillard and Emmanuel Kwaku Oboe

May their souls rest in perfect peace.
May the ancestors smile upon them. And may their spirits
continue to watch over our earthly journeys.

Contents

Preface

For many teachers, researchers, and leaders, an often unspoken but present desire in our academic lives is to live with the deepest of intimacy, a desire to live close to and with reverence for the life that is within and around us. However, given the weight of history and the meaning that both spirituality and Black womanhood have within the spheres of academic life, speaking the truth of their impact and their grace too often renders women of color afraid of the risks involved in embracing spirituality in our academic lives—and sometimes, even more afraid *not* to.

On spiritual strivings: Transforming an African American woman's academic life applies a spiritual imagination and cultural framework to the examination of African American women's academic lives and to the following questions. How does the embrace of spirituality affect what we, as African American women do (and might do) in our academic lives? How does what we do in our academic lives affect and shape who we become as African American women and what we then can offer the world as a result of these lives?

These questions draw much inspiration from the brilliance of esteemed African American intellectual and activist W. E. B. Du Bois (1989). I remember my first encounter with his life-changing book, *The souls of black folk*. It was in the late 1970s and I was taking an American history course at Central Washington University, located in a small rural town in my home state of Washington. In the course, we were allowed to choose an author whose work we believed had made a major historical impact on American education. And as an education major with a growing Black consciousness, I chose to study the work of W. E. B. Du Bois. Now, nearly thirty-five years later as

I prepared this manuscript, I revisited Du Bois's *The souls of black folk*. And I rediscovered the same excitement I felt then, that of reading an intellectual work where the author so accurately and powerfully names the places, spaces, and conditions of Black people in a way that had been unarticulated (and maybe unarticulatable) for so many. But this time, I was struck by the the relevance and timelessness of what he called the "spiritual strivings" of African Americans, our ongoing desire and quest to bring a sense of clarity to what he describes as both our African and American souls. And like many women scholars of color, finding balance between, within and among our multiple identity positions in the varying global and local contexts and spheres where we work is a long-standing challenge in our academic lives.

Du Bois articulated two strivings that I use as the deep structure of this book. The first was his desire to reconcile what he called our *double consciousness*, that is, for the "[Negro] to merge [her] double self into a better and truer self (p. 3)." The second striving specifically speaks to a pan-African desire, and is articulated in this quote from Du Bois (1986): "As I face Africa, I ask myself: What is it between us that constitutes a tie that I can feel better than I can explain?" (pp. 639–670). In the pages of this book, I seek to provide both a context and content for examining that question and, theoretically and experientially, providing a response to both of these strivings. I explore the way that a conscious centering of spirituality and Black feminist thought responds to Du Bois's strivings, that is, both to the everyday realities of double consciousness and to a strong desire for reconciliation in the souls of African Americans generally and African American women in particular. Examining the spiritual centering of teaching, research, and service from African and Black feminist frameworks, I seek to illuminate the tranformative possibilities that lie in making more conscious connections to Africa in our work, and the process by which such connections can transform an academic life into one whose purpose is healing and service through teaching and research.

In both the contexts and the content, this book explores multiple intersections and cultural spaces. Disciplinarily, its context and content is positioned between and within the fields of education, African American and African studies, Black feminist studies, and spiritual studies. Geographically, the research that grounds it lies primarily between and within Ghana, West Africa and the United States. Rhetorically and representationally, it is structured between and within the traditions and forms of narrative, poetry, storytelling, essay, and qualitative research. Grounded in an African-centered and Black feminist standpoint, such a variety of representational styles begins to more closely gesture toward the confluence of a Black feminist aesthetic and African cultural ethos and toward modes of representation that have been little explored in the education literature. I make these moves for two reasons. First, the field of education has numerous studies about African American life and communities. On closer examination, however, one finds that it overflows with explanations of African American embodied "others," legitimized by the field as "real" descriptions of the way that our family histories, culture, religions, experience, and aspirations create the contexts and people we, as African and African American people have become. And most tragically, the voices of African American women are all too often silenced and absent from these explanations of the very communities of which we are so deeply a part.

Second, given our training and academic preparation as researchers, teachers, and scholars, we all too often gaze and burrow into the lives of others in pursuit of our projects, but too seldom turn the gaze on ourselves, our work and the reasons we do what we do. This book is an attempt to bring a critical gaze to my own academic life and work, embracing the messiness, tensions, and complexities involved in writing myself and other African women scholars into the text with the sort of intellectual and spiritual integrity that further explicates Du Bois's spiritual strivings and firmly characterizes and resonates with "the souls of Black folk," most specifically Black womenfolk. For me, writing that is both theoretical and biographical can also provide a glimpse of ourselves and the transformational power of the spirit in our lives as African American women academics, illuminating the spirituality that is all too often rendered invisible or insignificant in (white) academe by virtue of our race, gender, and other identity positions and the "isms" others embrace. As issues of diversity increase, such alternative ways of being academic are needed that include the cultivation of skills, knowledges, and cultural understandings that enable us to be healers through the very acts of teaching, research, and service.

Finally, I use multiple feminist and artistic rhetorical styles and topics, moving beyond simply "discussing" spirituality as transformational possibility in an academic life to exploring these themes at the level of representation in an African American woman's academic life. Because we live and work in contexts that have been structured and dominated by a mostly Western, white, male, and capitalistic hegemony, my hope is that the reader may come to know ways of being, thinking, and doing that may encourage her or him to attune not just to their mind, but also to their spiritual reservoirs in teaching, research, service, and leadership. It is hoped that these explorations of the "know-how" and "be how" of African and African American women's cultural understandings might inform all of our academic lives—and ultimately transform these lives into tools of service for life itself.

About five years after reading Du Bois's *Souls of black folk,* I read what I remember as my first Black feminist text, edited by three African American women whose work has been foundational to my intellectual and academic life: Gloria (Akasha) T. Hull, Patricia Bell-Scott, and Barbara Smith. The title of the book was *All the women are white, all the Blacks are men, but some of us are brave* (1982). Just hearing the words of that title has over the years provided strength and encouragement for me and countless other African American women as we attempt to speak truth to power in our academic lives. And inherently, these words also speak to several desires (maybe cautions) that I have for the reader of the book you hold in your hands.

First, the stories shared here are not metaphorical: They are recountings of *actual* occurrences. An excerpt from a written meditation in Chapter 5 stands as an example:

> You honored my family name
> On the front of the community center and preschool,
> And I became my parents, their parents, parents, parents,
> Those who, by virtue of the Blackness of Africa
> Were considered by some
> Not to be fully human . . . (p. 99)

What I am describing here is the story of the day I was enstooled as a Queen Mother in Ghana, West Africa and was given the name Nana Mansa II. The lines of the meditation speak to the actual events and experience of becoming a Queen Mother, of an African collective history: They are not a wish, fairy tale or something in the world of imagination. Given such groundedness, my desire for this book is this: that these stories actually create a spiritual connection with reader, that you *will* actually experience the day of my enstoolment, the courage of the women of Mpeasem, the peacefulness of meditations on the shores of Ghana and the ways they transform one's perspectives and ways of being and living an academic life. It is important to note that the personal nature of the experiences within the stories shared here are not important in and of themselves: Every person has an abundance of the gift of life's stories within us. But I am suggesting here that stories of the myriad of our experiences—of people, identities, places, and experiences—when carefully crafted by the teller and carefully heard by the listener, can open what Palmer (1998) so aptly and beautifully calls the inner landscape of an academic life. They can reveal meaning in our lives *that unfold only in the sharing*. They can provide us fruitful spaces of contemplation and reflection. And they can provide wisdom and knowledge, evidence and example of another way of being engaged in the life and work of teaching, research, and service.

My second desire for this book has to do with the importance of contemplating spirit in research, teaching, and leadership practice. While we cannot know in advance how the reading of any text will *inspire* (from Latin roots, meaning "to breathe into") us, some of what we already know and believe to be truth, the ways we behave, or how we are becoming may not survive intact after reading a particular text. This is certainly what both W. E. B. Du Bois and Akasha Hull, Patricia Bell-Scott, and Barbara Smith's books did for me. So my second desire is this: that you will also be changed or transformed by what is here, by your experience with this book. And this may not necessarily be *easy*. But when I turn to the sage wisdom of spirit, embodied in elders of African ascent, in the voices of the ancestors, and the sacred space of Africa (and Ghana particularly) and when they collectively say "All is well," I listen and I am reassured. They know. They've been there and done that. And their knowledge, arising from experience, is what I trust—and what I hope you will remember and take away from the reading.

Chapter 1 begins with an examination of the epistemological assumptions that have shaped my academic life and the lives of many African American women academics. I articulate how reality is known when based in the historical roots of Black feminist thought, embodying a distinguishable difference in cultural standpoint and contemporary contexts of oppressions and resistance for African American women. The notion of an endarkened feminist epistemology is put forth, implying a shift in the metaphors and ideologies that have been taken for granted in our academic lives and the spirit of our purposes and practices in research, teaching, and leadership. Chapter 2 takes up the task of articulating a spiritually grounded paradigm in the oft-contested cultural and intellectual discussion of how, as more research-ers of color enter the public discussion and spheres of educational research with alternative knowledge and realities, the research com-munity names our articulations of difference as somehow creating a problem or a "proliferation" of paradigms. The chapter concludes with a discussion of definitions and purposes of spirit within one's paradigm and the ways in which being spiritual is a legitimate frame through which to participate in the social and political struggles of the world, including those that we undertake in our academic lives.

Examining the notion of teaching and research as service is the focus of Chapter 3. Through the story of my work in building a pre-school in Ghana, West Africa, I examine the tensions, contradic-tions, struggles, and joys that are available to teachers and researchers when we shift our perspectives about the nature of our roles as teach-ers and researchers with/in the world. In light of these roles and within a spiritual framework, Chapter 4 takes up the rather taboo subject of death and dying and the ways that life and death might be perceived as one eternal research moment, always holding important insights and implications for the ability to see our teaching and re-search as spiritual engagements. We live in increasingly troubled times today, times when educational researchers and teachers are continu-ally called to examine and respond to issues such as violence in schools, inequitable and unjust characterizations of racial and ethnic differ-ence, increased poverty, and terrorism within our borders, regardless of our roles within the society. And as researchers and teachers, we are also called to "explain" the devastating effects that such issues are having in our communities and in our world and to make recommen-dations about how to end the devastation. Essentially, these are dis-cussions about life and death, discussions that are often difficult, complex, and emotional. And they may also not be adequately ad-dressed or resolved by the rationalistic, objective methodology and representations that we've traditionally held as "legitimate" forms of research and representation. Thus, Chapter 4 attempts to answer the following question: What kinds of spaces might be opened for more expansive understandings of research and teaching when we start from the premise that death is not an extraordinary event but instead part of the same continuum as the life we are living?

Chapter 5 focuses mainly on methodological practices as a part of a research life. Through the experience of becoming a Queen Mother in Ghana, West Africa, I explore what I call a methodology of surrender that seeks to embrace a research space where methods are both intimately meditative (that is, where we listen and heed the wisdom of the ancestors and the Creator) and faith filled (that is, where we are prayerfully attentive and grateful to the spiritual world and the Creator). Chapter 6 explores the importance (and the difficulties) of listening and being true to the voice within, amid the pressures of an academic life, as well as to the tensions of the multiple "sites" of our academic lives, whether in classrooms, research sites, or in service endeavors. Here, I also take up the responsibility we have as scholars to see the socialization process of young scholars as one of *invitation into a relationship* of and with teaching, research, and service. In this way, our academic lives are not only a transformational force for those seeking a future in our vocation, but can serve as a healing force in the present as well.

Chapter 7 is about coming to the place where beyond race, class, gender, and other identity positions, one can name one's essence as spirit, an identity where as Thich Nhat Hanh (2001) suggests, "my identity meets your identity in order to be possible" (p. 120). This chapter looks critically at the usefulness of sociocultural identities (particularly racial and gender identities) and explores Du Bois's notion of African American double consciousness when set against the African racial and cultural landscape of Ghana. The final chapter of the book takes us "full circle," opening in the slave dungeons in Elmina, West Africa. I discuss the ways that, embodied in practice, Du Bois's spiritual strivings may quite literally change our lives, moving us closer to our divine purposes—and possibly farther away from what we've known as the academic life that has been our journey so far.

Acknowledgments

I give thanks . . .

To the Creator, who graciously wakes me every morning to finish the work I have to do on earth;

to the ancestors, including my Dad, Grandpa Oboe, Grandma Miller, and my elder sister, Octavia, whose strength, perseverance, and creativity are my inheritance;

to the love of my life, my Henry, who is my rock, my soft place to fall, and the partner I always dreamed of and whom I now am blessed to dream *with*;

to my family on both sides of the water—Mom, Celeste, Judith, Mitch, Taylor, Andreas, Mom and Dad Oppong, and all the extended family, young and old, present and departed;

to Demetrius Johnson, whose constant encouragement to write this book so she "could have my book on her shelves" was just what I needed on those days when both the motivation and the wisdom were difficult to come by;

to Patti Lather, my dear friend and colleague who has been a part of this project from start to finish and who nourished my mind, body, and spirit in the hours spent over wine on the deck, discussing "the book";

to the doctoral students in my seminar on Ghana, for your thoughtful reading and critical response and dialogue to multiple drafts of this book: Daniel Finn, Hillary Hardt, Terry Husband, Jr., Edric Johnson, Danielle E. Woods, Gumiko Monobe, Tami Tuten, and Lynn Weaver: I appreciate and admire you all!

to my numerous friends, students, and others who supported and nourished this work;

to Margaret Grogan, series editor for the State University of New York's (SUNY) Women in Education series, and Lisa Chesnel, acquisitions editor at SUNY for their vision and support of this work;

and to the children and people of my West African village of Mpeasem, Ghana: You gave my academic life some new wings. Now we can really fly . . .

The author gratefully acknowledges Taylor and Francis (www.tandf.co.uk) for permission to use my previously published article: Dillard, C. B. (2000). The substance of things hoped for, the evidence of things not seen: Examining an endarkened feminist epistemology in educational research and leadership. *International Journal of Qualitative Studies in Education*, 13, 661–681.

The author also gratefully acknowledges Sage Publications for their permission to use the following previously published talk: Dillard, C. B. (2002). Walking ourselves back home: The education of teachers with/in the world. *The Journal of Teacher Education*, 53, (5), 383–392.

1

The Substance of Things Hoped For,
The Evidence of Things Not Seen

Examining an Endarkened Feminist Epistemology
in Educational Research and Leadership

The call for recognition of cultural diversity, a rethinking of
ways of knowing, a deconstruction of old epistemologies, and
the concomitant demand that there be a transformation in our
classrooms, in how we teach and what we teach, has been a
necessary revolution—one that seeks to restore life to a corrupt
and dying academy.

—bell hooks, *Teaching to transgress*

According to Stanfield (1993), "epistemological concerns in
cultural research in the social sciences cannot be divorced from concerns regarding the functions of culturally hegemonic domination in
knowledge production and dissemination and in the selections and
rewarding of intellectual careers" (p. 26). Additionally, the underlying understanding of the nature of reality and the forms of discourse
one employs (or is encouraged or permitted to employ) to construct
realities in research on leadership significantly impacts not only what
can be said and how it is said, but where it is said. Nowhere is this
truer than in the interpretation and representation of educational
inquiry, especially as we engage more artistic modes of research (Eisner,
1979; Greene, 1978; Walker, 1996; Yenne-Donmoyer & Donmoyer,
1994). As we see a gradual "opening up" of the uses of Black vernacu-
lar and more indigenous references in pop culture representations in
theater, music, and the like (although still primarily controlled and
attended by predominantly white audiences), it seems reasonable to

1

assume that the educational leadership research community might also be ready to examine more culturally indigenous ways of knowing research and enacting leadership in the academy. In this way, such voices are provided legitimation, not of their existence, but as analytic, conceptual, and representational tools that explicate deep meanings of the very bases of educational research and leadership: its ontologies, epistemologies, pedagogies, and its ethical concerns.

I will argue here that when we begin to move beyond race/ethnic and gender as biological constructions to more culturally engaged explanations of being human, and when we seek to examine the origins of such knowledge constructions as to the very nature of how reality is known (its patterns of epistemology) (1), we will find that what constitutes knowledge depends profoundly on the consensus and ethos of the community in which it is grounded. Given the shifting demographics and recent interest in "multicultural" communities and people of color, it is not only an ethical imperative for researcher/leaders, but also a compelling possibility to engage a differing metaphor of research, one that profoundly disrupts the idea of neutral relationships and structures in inquiry and points instead to the complex nature of research when it maintains allegiance and substantive connections to the very communities under study. Thus, alternative epistemological truths are *required* if educational researchers and leaders are to be truly responsible, asking for new ways of looking into the reality of others that opens our own lives to view—and that makes us accountable to the people, interests, and needs of whom we study.

As an African American feminist scholar, I will examine in this chapter what I call an endarkened feminist epistemology. In defining an endarkened feminist epistemology, I have deliberately sought language that attempts to unmask traditionally held political and cultural constructions/constrictions, language that more accurately organizes, resists, and transforms oppressive descriptions of sociocultural phenomena and relationships. In this vein, Asante (1988), Morrison (1993), Ngugi Wa Thiongo (1986) and others have suggested that language has historically served—and continues to serve—as a powerful tool in the mental, spiritual, and intellectual colonization of African Americans and other marginalized peoples. They further suggest that language itself is epistemic, that it provides a way for persons to understand their reality. Thus, in order to transform that reality, the very language we use to define and describe phenomena must possess instrumentality: It must be able to *do* something toward transforming particular ways of knowing and producing knowledge (2).

Therefore, in contrast to the common use of the term "enlightened" as a way of expressing the having of new and important feminist insights (arising historically from the well-established canon of white feminist thought), I use the term "endarkened" feminist epistemology to articulate how reality is known when based in the historical roots of Black feminist thought, embodying a distinguishable difference in cultural standpoint, located in the intersection/overlap of the culturally constructed socializations of race, gender, and other identities, and the historical and contemporary contexts of oppressions and resistance for African American women. Such attention to the epistemological levels of research and leadership also implies a shift in the research metaphors and an uncovering of the ideologies that we have taken for granted, those that have traditionally left unproblematized our goals, purposes, and practice in educational research. In order to articulate an endarkened feminist epistemology, it is important that I first address the shifting ground of educational research and the prevailing metaphors that have [mis]guided us in our research endeavors.

Changing Metaphors, Changing Ideologies: The Shifting Cultural Ground of Research

All research is social construction and a cultural endeavor. A major contribution of feminist, ethnic, and cultural studies to the educational research community has been the reframing of the research endeavor as an *ideological* undertaking, one deeply embedded within the traditions, perspectives, viewpoints, cultural understandings, and discourse style of the researcher (Dillard, 1995; James & Farmer, 1993; Lather, 1986; Packwood & Sikes, 1996; Scheurich & Young, 1997, Stanfield, 1993). Packwood & Sikes (1996) argue convincingly that these ideologies are reflected in the metaphors that we use to conceptualize both the processes and the epistemological bases of research. Ironically, however, they suggest that even in the current plethora of narrative accounts of research (see Casey, 1995 for a comprehensive

review of narrative research in education), the most pervasive metaphor characterizing the final product (the research paper or published
article) is still that of research as recipe. They suggest further that

> this is not only an implicit metaphor, it is also an implicit myth. The
> metaphor is that the process of research is to follow a recipe, and the
> myth is that this is the truth. These are illusions that researchers per-
> petuate. We perpetuate them by the way we present our final research
> texts and by the way we carefully delete the voice of the researcher,
> our own voice, from the text. (p. 336)

We can see from the metaphor of research as recipe, that the
relationship between the researcher (as "knower") and the researched
(as "known" or to be known) is one of detachment: The researcher
is set apart from the subject (the recipe) in order that knowledge (the
final outcome) is "objective." While much has been written on the
virtues and pitfalls of positivistic quantitative social science, one could
argue that much qualitative work also rests on similar conceptions of
"truth." I would further add that regardless of research paradigm, if
educational research is to truly change or transform, it will only be
because we are in the midst of a "far-reaching intellectual and spiritual revisioning [and articulation] *of reality and how we know it*" (Palmer,
1983, p. xvii, emphasis mine). In other words, a transformation at the
epistemological level.

From my standpoint as an African American woman, moving
away from such a metaphor is critical, not simply as a move against
objectivity or one "right way" to engage in educational research. At
its episteme, it is for me a move away from the fundamentally
wrongheaded assumptions that undergird such a metaphor in my work
and the work of others, and toward a recognition of my own African-
centered cultural identity and community. This *necessitates* a different
relationship between me, as the researcher and the researched, between my knowing and the production of knowledge. This is also
where Black feminist knowledge (3) provides an angle of vision from
which to construct an alternative version of this relationship and a
new metaphor in educational research, one that moves us away from
detachment with participants and contexts and their use as "ingredi-
ents" in our research recipes and toward an epistemological position
more appropriate for work within such communities.

Thus, a more useful research metaphor arising from an endarkened feminist epistemology is *research as a responsibility*, answerable and obligated to the very persons and communities being engaged in the inquiry. As the purpose of this paper is to articulate an endarkened feminist epistemology, the metaphor of research as a responsibility is a central assumption—and an invitation to the reader to become aware of multiple ways of knowing and doing research available to those serious enough to interrogate the epistemological, political, and ethical level of their work. It is also the intent to enter and hopefully push forward Scheurich and Young's (1997) challenge toward a "lively discussion" about the "racial" in our research in two important ways. First, by placing the narratives of African American women at the center of this discussion of an endarkened feminist epistemology and articulating this epistemological position through these voices. Second, through illuminating the important meanings of the metaphor of research as responsibility in the enactment of an endarkened feminist epistemology.

Enacting Representation: Narrative Research as Cultural Ideology

Engaging an endarkened feminist epistemology has strong implications for the ways in which written texts are displayed and discussed. I have chosen in this chapter to explore the possibilities of narrative representations called life notes (Bell-Scott, 1994). Seen as a part of the body of research literature commonly known as narrative research, life notes refer broadly to constructed personal narratives such as letters, stories, journal entries, reflections, poetry, music, and other artful forms. However, as a form of narrative, life notes may be seen as embodying the meaning and reflections that consciously attend to a whole life as it is embedded in sociocultural contexts and communities of affinity. How such meaning is represented takes on importance here, with life notes holding the common trait of being relatively "unedited, uncensored, woman talk" (Bell-Scott, 1994, p. 13). An important assumption guiding this representational move is that African American women's "theory" has not been broadly utilized in mainstream educational research, even as it has been continually and constantly constructed and utilized within African American communities and contexts to give sense and meaning to one's life (Brown, 1988; Gordon, 1990; hooks, 1989; Some, 1994). Finally, I suggest that

African women's voices embodied in life notes can be seen as special-ized bodies of knowledge which, while legitimate and powerful, have been excluded from the reified bodies of knowledge and epistemologi-cal roots undergirding most social science research literature and prac-tice. This has led to the expression, self-definition, and validation of Black female understandings and knowledge production in alternative sites, that is, in music (such as in the African American blues tradi-tions), poetry, literature, and daily conversations, to name just a few (Hill Collins, 1990). I made the choice to represent data in this way to at least begin to gesture toward the confluence of the aesthetic, female, cultural sensibilities that are often stifled in traditional modes of representation and discourses, mostly because they require (but rarely receive) translation from one cultural context to the other, which de-naturalizes, reduces, and diminishes their richness and meaning. Fur-ther, the attempt within these narratives is to illustrate the relationships of power, the contexts of opportunity (or lack thereof), and to highlight the epistemological roots and their consequent local meanings in my life and in the lives of Black women researchers more generally.

In this chapter, I enact what one of Lightfoot's (1994) partici-pants, Katie Cannon, refers to as the "epistemological privilege of the oppressed" (p. 59): I speak truth to research and leadership as it is known by three prominent African American women leader/research-ers. The hope through utilizing life notes as a form is that readers of these texts will experience them as "overheard conversations, in ad-dition to actual literary texts" (Bethel, 1982, p. 180), conversations that embody a particular and explicit standpoint. In this way, these narratives may be viewed as at least part of the "evidence of things not seen," demystifying African American feminist ways of knowing, in moments of reflection, relation, and resistance: Black women's spaces where one can know who we are when we are most us.

Data were collected primarily through the use of interview, but also through the analysis of texts and written documents produced by three African American women. The first narrative is that of a graduate student in her second year of socialization and course work toward a doctoral degree in higher education administration. The second is that of a secondary school principal in an urban school district. The final narrative is autobiographical, written by me, as a college-level administrator at a predominately white university. Mul-tiple rhetorical styles are used to represent these women's voices in narratives. Although this representational move is mine alone, it was done in an attempt to both mirror and honor the style and substance of the data as it was shared with me. However, the reader should keep in mind a major purpose of this chapter: to explore, at the level of representation an endarkened feminist epistemology. In other words, in what is literally and metaphorically the chapter's center, I enact the ways that narrative research texts about research, teaching, and leadership are also cultural ideology, through three narrative life notes, positioned not as Other but as center, given "a society full of institutionalized and violent hatred for both [our dark] skins and [our] female bodies" (Bethel, 1982, p. 178). It is precisely at this point of representation, when the pressures to conform to the "norms" of "proper" scientific research are most difficult to resist that I seek to recognize the cultural genesis and meanings of the lives of African American women researchers and to disrupt and unsettle the taken-for-granted notions surrounding the very goals and purposes of educational research.

Life Notes Narratives: Three Voices

Narrative One: The Opening (4)

Where the road goes from paved to gravel is the place where my life is
Right in that spot, that line, that crack—
    There is the wormhole of who I be.

I be me in that space
    Dark and quiet—

And Whole—
Wholly me and made of all that is me
Journeying to the edges
    Spilling over to pavement or gravel—

Sustaining this entity through movement and talk
Folding into itself facing attack
Turning out onto the street facing struggle
Being me
    Being Whole
        Being me again

Ever re-creating
    clarifying
    pushing the edges
So that this Third Space
    between paved and gravel becomes . . .

and Becomes more than a crack (break yo' mama's back)
          a line (problem of the twentieth century)
          a spot (see it run)

    but Becomes . . .

and is becoming   whole (philosopher)
          integrated (transgressive)
          critical (-ly important)
          VOICED (heard)

Narrative Two: Leading with her life: A day in the life of a Black woman high school principal

I grew up here in Easely, right over in the South district. At that time there weren't too many of "us" [African Americans] so I knew everyone in the city who was Black. Schools? I went to Catholic schools all my life—even college! That's funny to me because even though I went to Catholic schools, and I wore a uniform, and was taught by the nuns and things, I actually got a really good education. It was about the only way to get an integrated education in Easely, especially in the 1950s. And that was important to my parents.

My Dad was an eighth-grade graduate and one of the first African American barbers on the Easely-to-Chicago train route. My Mom had two years of college. She was a teacher, too. My oldest sister went to college in the convent, and the other one still is a practicing nun. My brother, who's only ten months younger than me is the only one of us kids who didn't go to college. Education was really a priority for my family. Getting an education was important. My Dad used to say that we had to do better [than our white counterparts] because we're never good enough and we'll never be good enough. An education would help us to deal with that.

My Daddy used to make us sit there and watch the news, for hours. At first we wanted to go run the streets with our friends, but then it got really interesting. It got real. We discussed those things at the dinner table. We knew there was racism here in Easely, too, but it didn't take the same form. It was much more subtle. That's why my parents put such emphasis on getting a good education, to better prepare us to combat the racism we might face . . .

You may not know it, but I'm a teaching principal. It's really unusual but I did it because I'm not gonna take just anyone into my school. Yeah, it means a lot more work for me. But I did it because those available for the position in the surplus pool were less than desirable. And there weren't any [Black] folk in the pool either. The only way to get around that is not to open it up. So I started out just teaching one semester. Now I've been teaching for three years. It's just one of those things that you have to do with this job. And you know something? It shuts the faculty up. They can't say I don't know anything about the plight of teachers. . . .

I came to the district a long time ago. At that time Rosefield was all white. When they sent me here the school was more than 50 percent minority. That's part of the reason I'm here. My *promotion* [emphasis added] was that I was brought here to Rosefield to clean up this *mess* [emphasis added]. And it was a mess. But now [two years later] we're doing a lot better. But we're changing. The ninth-grade class is about 60 percent white again and I think this is a trend. Eventually, I'll be reassigned somewhere else. The community, the teachers, they will want a white principal again. That's just the way it is. You just have to go with it . . .

I don't need to have my own children because I've got 1,000 of them five days a week, six hours a day. There was this one student— she didn't do very well her first few years. She'd been in foster home after foster home. Finally, I got her into the Upward Bound program. Then she was selected as a Natural Helper. After a while, she began to really get into her classes. But then she would be disappointed when she got her report card. Her cumulative GPA was so low and as a senior, she thought she couldn't catch up. But I kept pushin' her. Her last two quarters she got a 4.0. For graduation, I got her a gift certificate to a local department store. She actually went on to university, over there where you are, I think! You need to look her up! . . .

You know, as the principal, I go through all of the report cards and write notes on them before they are given to the kids—all 800 of them. All students with 4.0 get stamps saying "excellent"—and I write a little note, too. All kids with a 3.0 get a different stamp. And all the Black kids with a 3.0 get another special stamp. And then any kid who shows improvement gets a stamp, too! It takes me a long time, but it's important to recognize their achievements . . .

[She answers the telephone.] Yes. Rachelle Smith? This is Gloria Natham, the principal at Rosefield, Issac's school. Well, Ms. Thomas. I need to tell you that we were under the understanding that Issac picked up his transcripts [from his previous school]. We have been working with the counselor. He's been playing around and now since he didn't register, we can only get him a second- and third-period class. He was up here on registration day, but he didn't bother to go through registration. So this is what we're gonna do. He's gonna go immediately into the Learning Assistance Center (a special student study hall/tutorial). He came in here playing and we need to let him know that we take his education seriously. He will also have a con-tract. That means he signs in every day with each of his teachers and a progress report is sent to you every other week. Now, Issac does not need any help or encouragement with ways to help him make excuses. If he has a dental appointment or something, then you need to write him a note. But we do not excuse students for sleeping in or being late. And we do not have to accept all of his notes either. See, it's just like a job. They only let you be absent or late one or two times and then you're out. So, I'll get the counselors together so we can make him a schedule . . . He'll have the progress report and attendance card every week. He [now] knows that you know he has it so there's none of that. See, what we're trying to do here is get him through school. Bye-bye . . .

Some people grumble because I really don't have an open-door policy. I don't want folks to visit me like they'd visit their hairdresser or their psychiatrist. I don't have time for that. I have better things to do with my time. They should know how to teach . . . I have been into each teacher's class during the first two weeks of classes. I just want to see what they're doing. When I came to Rosefield, the kids weren't in class. They were walking the halls. And almost every kid walking the halls were Black and Hispanic kids. They'd still be there happy as clams if we didn't get after them and the teachers whose class they were supposed to be in. Now the halls are clean and there are more of our Black and Asian and Hispanic kids in those higher-level classes. Part of the reason is that you're standing right in their faces [some of the traditional white teachers]. That kind of presence helps them to realize that you're not letting them off the hook. They've got to teach all of the kids . . .

I just put my foot down. If it's not good for kids, it's not good for Rosefield. I just say this is what we did and why we did it. It's as simple as that. But I have very good relationships with the [teacher's union]. I talk with them a lot! One of the guys named William Dudley, ya know, he's Black. And he just tells me the law. He came out here to Rosefield last year and came to some interesting perceptions himself [about what Natham sees as "old guard" faculty]. But what that means is that it puts us, on one hand, as friends. We're usually not in adversarial roles. But sometimes we are. But no matter whether it's positive or negative, you always wonder if the grievance or issue would be the same if you were a white principal. It's hard."

Narrative Three: A memorandum of understanding

To: Those who want to know at least part of the reason why Black women leaders might have an "attitude" in the academy

FROM: Author #2

RE: Some Real Colleague Blues (5)

DATE: April 1995
         I am looking for real colleagues
         I am looking for real, honest colleagues.

Not folk who assume from jump street that I've arrived in the Dean's office or the academy solely because of affirmative action, but folk who don't think that my leadership and teaching, particularly at a "prestigious" university, requires an extraordinary explanation for my being there.

I am looking for real honest colleagues who assume that my ways of being (my culture), my ways of knowing (my theory), and my ways of leading (culturally engaged) are not any less rigorous or righteous or real than their own but instead a place from which I center and make sense of my work as an African American woman. These real colleagues do not see a conflict between theory and cultural/experiential explanations as principles that guide thought and action, but recognize that it is that sort of didactical framing that inherently continues to advance a traditionally racist and sexist agenda, particularly in leadership and educational research.

In other words, I am looking for colleagues who do not believe that the bell curve really exists.

I am looking for real honest colleagues. Colleagues who are comfortable enough with their own constructions of their own humanity to respect mine. Who aren't scared of talking about the ways that racism, or classism, or sexism, or homophobia shape our decisions about policies and programs within education. Folk who know that those are the very conversations that will breathe life into an academy that thrives on reproducing privilege and inequality at every turn.

I am looking for good honest colleagues who will not ask the question: "What is it like to be a Black woman administrator? Oh yeah, I've got about five minutes," but instead will, over a glass of wine, cup of coffee, or a meal (and as a *regular* ongoing part of their lives), engage in the *reciprocal* dialogues and struggles necessary to actually hear my response—the blood, sweat, and tears, as well as the joy, the sensuality, the hopefulness, the spirit-filled nature of my being in and choosing administration as part of my academic life.

I am looking for colleagues who will understand why many Black women do not separate our "academic" work from the rest of our life's work, from advocacy work on behalf and in the very communities of color and women who nurture us, who take us in, who patch us up after what feels like a lifetime of struggle to survive the often brutal realities of the professoriate. We are intimately connected to our communities and must give homage to those whose work it has been to sit with us, talk with us, feed us, bandage us up, hug us, and remind us of the legacy of strong women and men of color who have come before us. It is only then, after we have been "pushed back to strength" as sister Gloria Wade Gayles would say, that our communities of care send us away from these home places, better and stronger advocates for the struggle of opportunity and human rights, especially in educational contexts.

I am looking for colleagues who can see that there are deep connections between being Black academics and leaders, mothers and lovers, and researchers and scholars that informs our work. These colleagues must recognize too that inherent in being one of the too few sisters who have successfully navigated a way through the maze of higher education leadership, I have a higher moral responsibility that transcends being widely published in the top journals, beyond being "politically correct." In other words, women leaders of color and consciousness, while fully cognizant of and attentive to the requirements of tenure, promotion, and a scholarly life must also pay attention in our research, teaching, and leadership to Alice Walker's call for "each one to pull one [or more]."

In this vein, I am particularly looking for some leadership colleagues who "don't believe you're ready for a promotion to full-time associate dean," but two months later, after learning that I am a finalist for a deanship at a prestigious private university, suddenly discover my enormous talent and value to the institution. "An associate deanship is yours if you'd like it . . ."

Yeah, I am looking for some real honest colleagues.

I am yearning for some honest colleagues who know there is no such thing as an acceptable joke about race or gender or sexual orientation/affiliation and other honest colleagues who will "go off" without my being there;

I am seeking some I-am-equally-responsible-for-engaging-and-dialoging-in-the-most-honest-ways-I-can kinds of colleagues;

I am looking for, searching for (and in some cases, I am fortunate enough to have found) honest colleagues who are not intimidated or confused by the power and magic of women of color, who choose to be leaders. Especially articulate, bright, well-published, successful, gorgeous, connected, righteous Black women intellectual leaders who do not want to be rendered invisible in order to be accepted or acceptable in higher education. Do you know any colleagues like that?

The Substance of Things Hoped For: Theorizing Through an Endarkened Feminist Epistemology

You know where the minefields are . . . there is wisdom . . . You are in touch with the ancestors . . . and it is from the gut, not rationally figured out. Black women have to use this all the time, of course, the creativity is still there, but we are not fools . . . we call it the 'epistemological privileges of the oppressed.' How do you tap that wisdom—name it, mine it, pass it on to the next generation?

—S. L. Lightfoot, *I've known rivers*

These life notes provide a glimpse of the complexity of issues, identities, and politics that influence and shape particular conceptions and worldviews, and ultimately our lives as educational leaders and researchers. The intention here is not to present Black woman as victimized, unable or unwilling to recognize even our own complicity at times, especially at times when we resist "talking back" within the racist, sexist, and homophobic institutions where we work. It is further not the intention to present ourselves and our lives as "always acting from the position of powerlessness that white supremacy defines as our place" (hooks, 1995, p. 269). The legacies raised up in life note narratives—of precious mentors, mothers, comrades, and colleagues—suggest a strong historical ethos of commitment to transformative work through our research, teaching, and leadership, in honor to named communities of affinity and support. The final intention here is not to present race/ethnicity or gender as being essentialist, unchangeable or immovable. Instead, these positionalities must be seen as shifting and dynamic sets of social relationships that embody a particular endarkened feminist epistemological bases. Through utilizing multiple and complex representations, our ability to understand, construct, and negotiate between and among these multiple relations and realities can continue to unfold (Omi and Winant, 1986, McCarthy & Critchlow, 1993).

While these narratives offer versions of feminists and feminisms often unheard, they also articulate a conscious struggle in our attempt to do as Golden suggested: To "fess up" to the ambiguity often tied up in the chasm between biological/material and ideological/epistemological definitions of feminism, its constitutive theories and elements, and the complexity and range of representation and responses. However, an inclusive and transformative possibility of any/all feminist thought must fundamentally take into account the special and particular ways of seeing that Black and other marginalized female scholars bring to the knowledge production process, not as biological constructions but as historical, political, and cultural constructions, under constant and vigilant negotiation, and conceptualized to disrupt at least, and possibly "to dismantle the master's house" (Lorde, 1984, p. 112).

While there is no easy way to analyze these narratives, embodied within them are specialized knowledges that theorize a dismantling standpoint of and for African American women and that encompasses a coherent and dynamic epistemology: A place from which to theorize the leadership and research realities of Black women through situating such knowledge and action in the cultural spaces out of which they arose. Thus, in articulating an endarkened feminist epistemology and a new metaphor for research (as responsibility), I first examined patterns and themes that were found in common between the three narratives and placed those in the context of the literature on Black feminist/womanist thought, and also my own experiences and research findings as an African American woman leader and scholar. Then I raised several questions that helped me to do two things: (1) to conceptualize, theoretically ground, put forth alternative methodology and representational moves around which I could arrange these African American women leader's voices, articulating an endarkened feminist epistemology, and; (2) to offer broadened understandings for those in the research community who engage inquiry around culture and the often slippery constructs of race, ethnicity, and gender—and who find their current epistemological positionings and more widely know research traditions unpalatable. The questions were these: Does the multiplicity of our modes of knowing representationally suggest a similar multiplicity in our understanding of the very nature of the realities of leadership? Said another way, are there patterns of epistemology that can help us to decipher the patterns of leadership lives, those situated political struggles and personal passions that lie at the nexus of scholarship and activism? For African American women leader/researchers living within our highly racist, sexist, and class-conscious society, how do we use experiences of racism, sexism, and other oppressions to inform our research as well as our leadership? Might the discourses we employ—and their patterns of epistemology—differ from what is traditionally known or spoken as "academic"? If so, how are they different? Most important, what do particular standpoints make possible in educational inquiry and how might that assist the entire research community in conceptualizing our work beyond often simplistic, biological and didactic notions of identity, politics, and the like to more useful cultural ones? Said another way, how do the insights engaged in being and living as an African American woman leader/researchers open up new possibilities for the research and leadership community to see phenomena in new ways?

Given this analysis, what then are the assumptions of an endarkened feminist epistemology? Maybe more important, within a cultural view of narratives, what might such assumptions tell us about the partial, situated, nature of any claims to knowledge, given the dynamic shifts and even contradictory nature of research experiences and explorations of cultural identity?

Before discussing these assumptions, several caveats are in order. Fine (1992) suggests the pervasion of gender into predominately studies of gender differences may be safe within the context of education and particularly feminist research, but makes us deploy and legitimate essentialist understandings of gender and "reproduce dualities/beliefs about gender, sexuality, and race and ethnicity" (p. 8). Patricia Hill Collins (1990) suggests further that Black feminist ideology "does not mean that all African American women generate such thought or that other groups do not play a critical role in its production" (p. 22): Being biologically female (or male) does not automatically a feminist thinker make. Self-conscious, determined examination and struggle is often required in order to reject distorted and oppressive perceptions of women in general and African American women particularly, and to value human thought and action from self-defined standpoints. As Stanlee James (1993) further suggests, this consciousness work is itself a form of theorizing (6):

> Although Black women are often characterized as victims, theorizing is a form of agency that provides them with opportunities to learn, think, imagine, judge, listen, speak, write, and act—and which transforms not only the individual (from victim to activist, for example) but the community, and the society as well. (p. 2)

Such "theorizing" is confounded by the vigilant need for African American scholars and leaders not simply to study and read written texts, "but [to read] the situation we [are] in . . . to understand the necessity for studying the terrains of hierarchy and power and hypocrisy and authenticity" (Omolade, 1994, p. xii).

The contours, politics, and research implications for engaging an endarkened feminist epistemological bases and related ways of research need to be explicated, particularly for those seeking to engage research in more alternative ways. However, I want to be clear about the viewpoint forwarded here, recognizing the reductionistic, flattening problematics inherent in "outlining" the assumptions of an epistemological stance. First, I do not subscribe to substituting a dominating white male version of science with a Black female version, reinscribing the same positivistic view of science. The social critique that endarkened feminist assumptions engage is focused on the violence perpetrated in the universal generalization from the particular White male knowledge of the nature of reality to describe everyone's realities, including those Black and female. This brings me to the second point: There is a need to resituate our research endeavors in their cultural and historical contexts, to reclaim their personal and social roots or origins. Thus, the fundamental questions in research should not be whether one epistemological bases is logical (all cultural groups develop logical thought, albeit differently from one another). Rather, as Palmer (1983) suggests, the question should be

> Whose voice is behind the thought? What is the personal and communal reality from which that thought arises? How can I enter and respond to the relation of that [those] thinker[s] to the world? (p. 64)

As a Black feminist researcher, I utilize both African/African American and feminist literature in theorizing these assumptions, reflecting the representation (conceptual and epistemological) of elements of both traditions in articulating an endarkened feminist epistemology. While I draw heavily on Collins's (1990) core theories of Black feminist thought and Harding's (1987) elements of feminist psychology respectively, I have also drawn on Palmer's (1983) work on spirituality in education. While rarely mentioned in discussions of educational research and teaching (see Dillard, Tyson, and Abdur-Rashid (2000), for an examination of spiritual concerns in teacher education), spirituality is intimately woven into the ethos of an endarkened feminist epistemology. The convergence of these three bodies of literature, along with my examination of the narratives presented here, provide primary contexts for imagining and theorizing these assumptions.

Finally, as Stanfield (1993) suggested at the outset of this chapter: "Epistemological concerns in cultural research in the social sciences cannot be divorced from concerns regarding the functions of culturally hegemonic domination in knowledge production and dissemination and in the selections and rewarding of intellectual careers" (p. 26). Thus, articulating these assumptions of an endarkened feminist epistemology is important for a number of reasons: First, in raising awareness of the power relations played out in our academic careers as researchers; second, and more pragmatically, to provide guidance (and courage) to members of tenure committees, publication review board who may better recognize the "validity" of the work of African American women within and outside of the academy, based on these alternative set of assumptions; third and finally, to challenge the all too prevalent idea that there is a unitary way to know, do, and be in educational research endeavors.

Assumption #1: Self-definition forms one's participation and
  responsibility to one's community

From an endarkened epistemological ground, all views expressed and actions taken related to educational inquiry arise from a personally and culturally defined set of beliefs that render the researcher *responsible* to the members and the well-being of the community from which their very definition arises. For example, in the narrative of the principal, she talks passionately about being responsible to African American and other students of color particularly—and *students,* more generally. However, as she describes the motivation for that sense of responsibility, she takes us back to her childhood and he own schooling experiences as a source of self-definition.

According to Hill Collins (1990), while race and gender are both socially constructed categories fraught with problematics, one could argue that constructions of gender rest on clearer biological criteria than those under girding race (Appiah, 1992; Bell, 1992; Omi & Winant, 1993; West, 1993). However, while united by biological sex, women as a category do not construct the same meaning of woman, given distinct her stories, geographic locations, origins, cultures, and social institutions. While most feminist scholars would recognize and subscribe to at least some common experiences based in culturally engendered experiences of being female, the experiences are qualitatively different for those who stand outside the circle of "acceptable" women, most particularly African American women (King, 1988). This is not meant to suggest that an additive analysis is ever useful in educational research, that is, that the greater the multiplicity of oppressions, the purer the vision of group members on marginalization or subjugation. Instead, what is suggested is that the struggle for a self-defined feminist consciousness for African American women in our roles as scholars seems to require embracing both a culturally centered worldview (in this case African-centered) and a feminist sensibility, both necessary in embracing and enacting an endarkened feminist epistemological stance. Through such praxis, an alternative ideology and cultural meaning for research is articulated, one that reflects elements of both traditions, a both/and standpoint (Hill Collins, 1990) deeply rooted in the everyday experiences of African American women. In the narratives, even with the variability that was articulated in the unique individual versions of who we are as Black women researchers, coherence is realized in our collective refusal to be reduced to someone else's terms: To give voice to silenced spaces as an act of resistance.

Defining oneself in relation to one's cultural and social community also defines one's participation within that community, both one's connection and affiliation as well as one's responsibility. Thus, if one claims that one is *of* the group (that is, chooses to conduct research and makes assessments of claims to knowledge of the group, however distant or intimate those claims), there must be a simultaneous assessment of a person's character, values, motives, and ethics in relation to that group (7). In other words, regardless of the identity position claimed (e.g., Black, white, male, female, etc.), from an endarkened feminist epistemological standpoint, the researcher would necessarily and carefully examine their own motives, methods, interactions, and final research "reports"—and seek understanding and meaning making from various members of the social and/or cultural community under study. In essence, each of the three voices here unabashedly claimed an identity standpoint and cultural positionality as Black women (e.g., "I be me in that space/Dark and quiet—And Whole"). However, it is through the voice of the principal in narrative two that we can clearly see self-identity and responsibility to the students and staff at Rosefield, enacted in her refusal to allow "undesirable" teachers into her building and taking the vacant teaching position herself, increasing the number of African American teachers in the building.

This allowed her to create a self-definition—and a socially constructed definition as well among teachers—as an African American woman teaching principal. Such a definition formed both how she participated in the community of teachers, the manner that she would respond to that community, and maybe most important, the manner in which the community responded to her.

From an endarkened epistemological ground, all views expressed and actions taken related to educational inquiry arise from a personally and culturally defined set of beliefs that render the researcher *responsible* to the members and the well-being of the community from which their very definition arises: To know something is to have a living relationships with it, influencing and being influenced by it, responding to and being responsible for it.

Assumption #2: Research is both an intellectual and a spiritual pursuit, a pursuit of purpose

An endarkened feminist epist\emology draws on a spiritual tradition, where the concern is not solely with the production of knowledge (an intellectual pursuit) but also with uncovering and constructing truth as the fabric of everyday life (a spiritual pursuit). Thus the "theories" of knowing that have guided research as a value-free social science are directly challenged when an endarkened feminist epistemology is articulated, as suggested here by Hill Collins (1990):

> Alternative knowledge claims are rarely threatening to conventional knowledge. Such claims are routinely ignored, discredited, or simply absorbed and marginalized in existing paradigms . . . [However] much more threatening is the challenge that alternative epistemologies offer to the basic process used by the powerful to legitimate their knowledge claims. If the ideology used to validate knowledge comes into question, then all prior knowledge claims validated under the dominant model become suspect . . . The existence of an [endarkened] feminist ideology calls into question the content of what currently passes as truth and simultaneously challenges the process of arriving at that truth. (p. 219)

As suggested in the final narrative: "I am looking for colleagues who do not believe the bell curve really exists." African American women have historically and contemporarily addressed our multiple oppressions (personal and societal) through versions of spirituality (James, 1993; Lightfoot, 1994; Richards, 1980; Vanzant, 1996; Wade Gayles, 1995). However the educational research literature by or about African American women researchers/teachers' spiritual concerns, though often unnamed, are pervasive (see exemplars in Foster, 1990; hooks, 1994; Ladson Billings, 1994). While these works are deeply intellectual, several conditions or elements are embedded within their purpose that imply research as a spiritual pursuit. First, there is an explicit, very powerful sense of self in the role of researcher/teacher, directly linked to an explicit sense of purpose for whatever research moves are made. Second, there are often multiple levels of vulnerability in the research endeavor. An endarkened feminist epistemology enacts "stepping out on faith," whether traversing tenure and promotion, publication, unequal power relations or just being present in the academy, or being "pushed back to strength" as we heard in the narratives. Third, there is reciprocity and care apparent in the relationships of the research project, embodying three major components. The first component is the recognition that each individual is a unique expression of a common spirit inherent in all of life (James, 1993; Paris, 1995; Richards, 1980; Some, 1994; Vanzant, 1996; Wade-Gayles, 1995). Such spiritual concerns are articulated epistemologically in that value is placed on individual expressiveness; individual differences are not seen as detracting from but as enriching to an endarkened feminist epistemology, the foundations and processes of our work. We see an example of such expressiveness in the simple line from the poem/narrative: "There is the wormhole of who I be." The second component is that emotions are considered not only appropriate but necessary in determining the validity of an argument (Hill Collins, 1990). Last, developing the capacity for empathy in research is critical, for attempting to recognize the value of another's perspective, whether or not one agrees with that perspective. Simply put, perspectives have merit and standing simply because they exist, and our role as educational researchers becomes one of recognizing and embracing them as such. In this way, we are encouraged to welcome the conflict inherent in our diversity (of paradigms, methodology, representation), to live within its sometimes seeming ambiguity, and to develop the purpose in research of not just honoring our own version of the practice, praxis, and politics of research as truth, but to seek to honor the truth that is created and negotiated in and between ourselves, in relationship with one another as researchers.

Assumption #3: Only within the context of community does the individual appear (Palmer, 1983) and, through dialogue, continue to become

This endarkened feminist epistemological assumption suggests that dialogue is key in both conducting research and in assessing knowledge claims: That there is value in the *telling*, in invading those secret silent moments often unspoken, in order to be understood as both participating in and responsible to one another as researchers. Further, there is value in being connected, in seeking harmony and wholeness as a way to discern "truth." In the narratives presented previously, the intention was partially to raise up the evidence of things not seen in the lives of African American women in the academy, while concomitantly inserting our voices into the research community in dialogic ways that insist that we exist, with language giving form to an endarkened feminist epistemology. These narratives might be seen as a dialogic offering for members of the educational research community whose work may be informed by what are equally valid ways of inquiry and knowledge production, embodied in the wisdom and knowledge of Black women's lives.

A number of researchers (Asante, 1988; Morrison, 1993; Ngugi Wa Thiongo, 1986) point to the importance of instrumentality in the languages and discourses used to create relationships based on equality, that is, in dialogue that transforms or provides a new way to understand our reality and communal responsibility, as women researchers, teachers, and scholars of color. "Dialogue implies talk between two subjects, not the speech of a subject and an object. It is humanizing speech, one that challenges and resists domination" (hooks, 1989, p. 131). This is the sort of dialogue implied and desired in the third narrative "over a glass of wine, cup of coffee, or a meal . . . engage in the *reciprocal* dialogues and struggles necessary to actually hear my response—the blood, sweat, and tears, as well as the joy, sensuality, and the hopefulness, the spirit-filled nature of my being." Thus, through awareness of an endarkened feminist epistemology, all involved in the conversation can resist and challenge entrenched ways of thinking about their research lives, and provide news ways to "be" researchers.

*Assumption #4: Concrete experience within everyday life form the
criterion of meaning, the "matrix of meaning making"
(Ephraim-Donker, 1997, p. 8)*

In African American communities, what happens in everyday life to
individuals within the community is critical to "making sense" of
particular actions, expressions, experiences, and community life in
general. Hill Collins (1990) suggests that this underlies two aspects
of knowing that are particularly important to this fourth assumption
of an endarkened feminist epistemology: knowledge and wisdom. She
further elaborates:

> Women of color cannot afford to be fools of any type, for our
> objectification as the Other denies us the protection that white skin,
> maleness, and wealth confer. This distinction between knowledge and
> wisdom, and the use of experience as the cutting edge dividing them,
> has been key to [our] survival. In the context of race, gender, and class
> oppression, the distinction is essential. Knowledge without wisdom is
> adequate for the powerful, but wisdom is essential to the survival of the
> subordinate. (p. 208)

Thus, in our scholarship and research, African American women often
invoke our own concrete experiences and those of other women and
communities of color in our selection of topics for investigation and
for the methodologies that we engage (Hill Collins, 1990). We "study"
the concrete experiences and acts of African American or people of
color, while at the same time striving to understand and explicate the
wisdom contained in those meanings. As Hill Collins continues:

> These forms of knowledge allow for subjectivity between the knower
> and the known, rest in the women themselves (not in higher authori-
> ties), and are experienced directly in the world (not through abstrac-
> tions). (p. 211)

Thus, concrete experiences—uniquely individual while at the same
time both collective and connected—lend credibility to the work of
African American women engaged in transformative research and
inquiry, as well as suggest the presence of an endarkened feminist
epistemology which grounds such work.

Assumption #5: Knowing and research are both historical
(extending backwards in time) and outward to the world:
To approach them otherwise is to diminish their cultural and
empirical meaningfulness

An endarkened feminist epistemology both acknowledges and works against the "absent presence" of women of color from the shaping of the rules that have historically guided formal educational research, the system of knowledge production within higher education, and the meanings and legitimacy surrounding research processes. In other words, Black feminist thought, while not a part of the original canon of theories, rules, and perspectives that surround what gets perpetuated today as educational research broadly defined, attempts to both highlight what's missing from these definitions as well as to extend these definitions through the inclusion of African women's knowledge. However, important to this assumption of an endarkened feminist epistemology is that such omissions have lead to what Wynter (1992) and others aptly describe as a distorted empirical reality fundamentally based on inclusion and exclusion as a way to maintain white and male superiority and as an organizer for our hierarchical social structures in education and society (Ani, 1994; Appiah, 1992; hooks, 1989; James & Farmer, 1993; Stanfield, 1994).

The disciplines of Black and other ethnic studies and women's studies have opened the way for multiple theoretical and epistemological readings in the fields of educational research. A major contribution of these fields is that feminist and scholars of color (and those of us who identify as both) have argued that members of marginalized groups have unique viewpoints on our own experiences and provide a needed critique as well as an "endarkenment" on society as a whole (Anderson, 1993; Foster, 1990; Haraway, 1988; Ladson-Billings, 1994; Lorde, 1984). Such standpoints suggest that race, class, gender, and other identity formations are both origins and subjects of particular knowledges. Accordingly, a feminist standpoint "preserves the presence of the active and experiencing subject" (Smith, 1987, p. 105). Standpoint theory also recognizes that researchers and subjects are located in specific and particular positionalities (Gitlin, 1994; Tierney, 1994). Within and against these locations, researchers engage in social relationships with research participants, and the process and work of research acknowledges and embraces the presence of the researcher.

However, an unexpected outgrowth of this body of work has been both an increasingly monolithic notion of various cultural identity groups (Stanfield, 1993) and often essentialist notions of who is capable, based on their own life histories, to conduct research with/ in various populations. While I will argue vehemently that Black women as a cultural group "theorize" and embody extensive life experiences which, while diverse, shape a coherent body (and as we saw in the life notes), what I am attempting to advance here is the notion that, in educational research, such theoretical and conceptual standpoints are *cultural;* they are not inherent in one's biology:

> Talk of race is particularly distressing for those of us who take culture seriously. For, where race works—in places where 'gross differences' of morphology are correlated with 'subtle differences' of temperament, belief and intention—it works as an attempt at metonym for culture, and it does so only at the prices of biologizing what is culture, *ideology* [emphasis mine]. (Appiah, 1992, p. 45)

We must recognize that the forms of discourse and literatures that have defined the claim of an epistemological universality (that which the talk of "theory" inevitably implies), inhibits both our ability to examine with necessary clarity (not to mention attention to ethical and moral concerns) and to interpret the complexity of human cultural thought and action that we study in educational research. In short, researchers who accept the relevance of poststructural, postmodern, feminist, and critical race theories, have reason to be at least uncomfortable with extending these theories to contexts, peoples, methodology, texts, and work outside this tradition. In other words, one's epistemological basis for research must engage in relevant cultural understanding and "theorizing" that is informed by the insights of those experiencing the world as the very phenomena being explored.

Thus, when research work is engaged within the cultural, social, political, and historical milieu of its creation—from its epistemology to the research experience to its report—we stand to get closer to what Appiah (1992) calls a productive mode of reading, a space and a way of seeing that creates the opportunity to rethink the meaning of the whole experience of research as an epistemological and cultural text.

Assumption #6: Power relations, manifest as racism, sexism, homophobia, and so on structure gender, race, and other identity relations within research

Whether concerns over research legitimacy, tenure and promotion, publication, or professional acceptability, asymmetrical power relations, particularly as they influence the work of women in the academy, have been well studied and articulated (see Fine, 1992; Harding, 1987; Harris, 1990; James & Farmer, 1993). However, while African American women are more present in the academy today, the racist, sexist, and classist structures and belief systems around us remain relatively unchanged. The consequences of such stability are even more extreme when Black women seek to situate ourselves into spaces of feminist discourse only to find that:

> In a racist society like this one, the storytellers are usually white and so 'women' turns out to 'white women.' Why in the face of the challenges from 'different' women and from feminist method itself is feminist essentialism so persistent and pervasive? In my view, as long as feminists, like theorists in the dominant culture, continue to search for gender and racial essences, Black women will not be anything more than a crossroads between two kinds of domination, or at the bottom of a hierarchy of oppressions; We will always be required to choose pieces of ourselves to present as wholeness. (Harris, 1990, p. 589)

Thus, an endarkened feminist epistemology has as its research project the vigilant and consistent desire to "dig up" the nexus of racial/ethnic, gender, and other identity realities—of how we understand and experience the world as Black women. For feminist research to truly embrace such an epistemological stance, gender, race, class, and other constructed identities (what some have despairingly referred to as "personal experiences" versus research texts), as well as the experiences meanings within power asymmetrics (Harding, 1987) that have historically constructed and been constructed by unequal access and contexts of power for Black women are positioned at the center of the research project. As the student said in the first narrative: ". . . Sustaining this entity through movement and talk / Folding into itself facing attack / Turning out onto the street facing struggle / Being me / Being Whole / Being me again . . ." These stories, when shared and heard by White researchers are often unbelievable at worst, painful fodder for contexts of White guilt at best. However, these cultural ideologies are the exact stories that "endarken" the episte-mology at work, that expose the relations of power that disproportion-ately exclude how and what we know the world to be as Black women, how we know racism and sexism and identity politics influence and shape the contexts of our lives, in contrast to being told how they operate from perspectives outside of ourselves. But at the same time, an endarkened feminism seeks to resist and transform these social arrangements as well, seeking political and social change on behalf of the communities we represent as the purpose for research, versus solely the development of universal laws or theories for human behavior.

A Final Note

Race is the tar baby in our midst; touch it and you get stuck, hold it and you get dirty, so they say. But anyone who reads these [life notes] will discover only premeditated ruminations designed to cleanse, complete, and free. The aching honesty, the willingness to critique and unveil the mark . . . is testimony to the bounty we could all share if we tried as hard to see each other as we try not to, or to 'fess up' rather than be nice.

—M. Golden and S. Shreve, *Skin deep: Black women and white women write about race*

It is with more than a little trepidation that I commit these private conversations and their analysis to more public spaces, espe-cially in what seems often daunting and exclusionary dialogues around race, class, and gender in educational research generally and leader-ship, more particularly. Like other Black feminist scholars, I have come to know intimately the angst that Critchlow (1995) speaks of: the outsider-within position (Hill Collins, 1990), of being a Black women scholar, and like most, relying on formal academic training designed to encourage us to decontextualize our deeply raced/gendered/classed/sexualized lives and alienate ourselves from our communities, families, and even ourselves in order to do "legitimate" scholarship: Attempting to work within such sites is fraught with immeasurable contradictions and exaggerations.

In the Christian biblical tradition, the underlying scripture from which the title is taken (Hebrews 11:1) relates to the importance of faith: "Faith is the substance of things hoped for, the evidence of things not seen." While critical of racism and sexism in higher education and unexamined epistemological assumptions that pass as universal truths in educational research, one might suggest that, simply by continuing to believe that such a dialogue *might be possible and useful* is an exhibition of the extraordinary faith we still manage to have for the possibility of engaging our collective humanity, even in the academy. Thus, this chapter is dedicated to those who work diligently to transform these often alienating positionalities, to those who "theorize" African American lived realities in ways that shape a more radical and transformative feminist politic in educational research. Envisioning research as responsibility might just be one of the shifts we need.

2

What Is It and Where Does It Live?

Toward Defining Spirit Within a Research and Teaching Paradigm

Much has been said about research paradigms in light of the ever present issues of ethnicity, race, and difference (Dillard, 2000; Scheurich & Young, 1997; Tyson, 1998). While the published discussion focuses on the multiple and contested meanings of paradigms and how differences function within said paradigms, I believe it worthwhile, in light of the increasing interest in difference, to explore how the idea of the "proliferation" of paradigms is also being constructed and thought about from politically and culturally engaged perspectives. The first task is to clarify several terms/concepts that seem critical to a discussion of paradigm proliferation and its "meanings" for research and teaching. This includes unpacking the idea of paradigms and finding some clarity and location of my own scholarship trajectory in relation to the field, as well as my identity location as an African American woman researcher deeply interested in how culture and spirituality might serve critical roles in such a response. And even in the raising of the question of paradigm proliferation, I believe there is a subtle (and not so subtle) meaning behind the very notion and language of "proliferation" that carries exlusionary political intentions and implications, and thus, needs to be exposed. I will argue here that the discussion of the proliferation of paradigms is fundamentally a discussion of the power and politics of how we do research and how we represent our research findings. This brings a particularized paradox for scholars of color as we seek to imagine, create, and embrace new and useful paradigms from and through which we engage in educational research. Finally, I will suggest that for researchers of color in particular, there are deep and serious implications in choosing to embrace paradigms that resonate with our spirit as well as our intellect, regardless of issues of "proliferation."

A Paradigm Is, A Paradigm Ain't: Setting My Own Record Straight

I start my search for a clear definition of paradigm with Webster's dictionary (2001), which defines it as "a set of all the inflected forms of a word based on a single stem or root; an example serving as a model." Not much help there. So I turned to the all important *Handbook of qualitative research* (1994). In their article "Competing paradigms in qualitative research," Guba and Lincoln (1994), broaden that definition to include "the basic belief system or worldview that guides the investigator, not only in choices of method but in ontologically and epistemologically fundamental ways" (p. 105). They argue the historical reality of two incommensurable paradigms, quantative and qualitative. However, with the emergence and popularity of qualitative or naturalistic inquiry in the 1980s, they discuss in detail the distinctions within and among what now might be seen as the "Big Four" paradigms: positivism, postpositivism, critical theory et al., and constructivism. While the merits of each paradigm are not taken up here, Guba and Lincoln do suggest that these paradigms simply represent "the most informed and sophisticated view that its proponents have been able to devise, given the way they have chosen to respond to the three defining questions [of ontology, epistemology, and methodology]" (p. 108). However, and most important, they suggest that regardless of differences, the fundamental site of distinction is in the manner that each paradigm determines and values the *nature* of inquiry, an epistemological difference.

Okay, so back to my undergraduate days in logic class. If one's paradigm is one's worldview, and one's paradigm is fundamentally one's epistemology, then is one's worldview also one's epistemology? Something still didn't seem right: If the focus of the fuss is on the proliferation of paradigms, I want to know more precisely what one IS! Do I have one? Can I ever have one? Are paradigms only things that others create for me? Or can I create a paradigm too?

But the more I read about the notion of paradigms, the more I began to recognize that paradigms (and their proliferation) are not seen as a very favorable condition to many scholars these days: It seemed instead that, as researchers, we are very subtly encouraged to "ascribe" (or subscribe?) to a particular one of the Big Four paradigms—and conduct ourselves according to the theoretical precepts outlined within them. In fact, Guba and Lincoln (1994) provide a strong warning that one might do well to locate oneself within a paradigm and that "membership" would provide at least some protection from the paradigm "wars" that our field is engaged in fighting:

> A resolution of the paradigm differences can occur only when a new paradigm emerges that is more informed and sophisticated than any existing one. That is most likely to occur if and when proponents of these . . . [paradigms] . . . come together to discuss their differences not to argue the sanctity of their views. (p. 116)

So being a part of the Big Four paradigms was not enough: it also seemed necessary to have something—a worldview, an epistemology, *something*—that we could all agree on and work within. Maybe a sort of Rainbow Coalition? A United Nations of Research? Seriously speaking, my original question still remained: What the heck is a paradigm and how will a "we are the world" version help me understand the discussion about how it is multiplying out of control?

It was in looking at Patton's definition and description (as cited in Donmoyer, 1999) that I began to more clearly understand at least some of this paradigm confusion (at best) and the "real-deal" about paradigms at worst. He states:

> A paradigm is a world view, a general perspective, a way of breaking down the complexity of the real world. As such, paradigms are deeply embedded in the socialization of adherents and practitioners: Paradigms tell them what is important, legitimate, and reasonable. Paradigms are also normative, telling the practitioner what to do without the necessity of long existential or epistemological consideration. (p. 37)

Through Patton's definition, I see that there indeed is a connection between paradigm and worldview: Both are defined as guiding principles and beliefs about what research is and what it is not. While

hooks (2000) defines paradigm in relation to worldview as our "foundational ways of thinking and doing things that become habitual" (p.
177), it seems important to make a connection *between* paradigm and
worldview from an African- and woman-centered location. So I lean
on Richard's (1980) definition of worldview as a way to articulate this
view of what a paradigm is: *"The way in which a people make sense of
their surroundings; make sense of life and the universe"* (p. 4). Here then,
the definition of a research paradigm becomes the way in which scholars, teachers, and thinkers articulate their sense of life around them,
make sense and order of the universe. Such an African worldview and
paradigm is conceived as a unified spiritual whole, that is, that one's
selfhood is understood and constituted as body, mind, *and* spirit and
affirmed in relationship to both one's group and to one's Creator. This
is in contrast to ways in which traditional research paradigms have
been constructed, where the relationship of the researcher to their
surroundings and those in the surroundings are too often dichotomous
and oppositional, especially in the relationships of cross-ethnic/cul-
tural research. While an African-centered viewpoint would suggest
that educational researchers make sense of their research worlds in
holistic terms, the Big Four paradigms are the outcome of a traditionally Western and European worldview that, by its nature, must cat-
egorize and separate in order to deem one paradigm good and the
other bad. By nature, such a worldview also attempts to destroy the
"bad" ones in order to have one or more sanctioned paradigms that
become the "best ones." But the ontological and epistemological underpinnings of how we even come to have the Big Four paradigms
seem to be totally absent (and thus rendered unimportant) in the
public discussion of what a paradigm is and is not. However, from an
African-centered worldview and paradigm, locating my own work
within the Big Four paradigms is not necessarily critical to either
legitimate or understand its content. Contrarily, I believe that every
worldview generates a set of definitional and cultural principles—and
that our scholarship is best explained or understood with those
definitions as the reference points for understanding.

Patton's definition of paradigms also helps me to see that our
near obsession with these structures called paradigms is also deeply
attached to our notions of politics and our use (and abuse) ultimately
of power. Worldviews are not innocent. Articulated in the principles

of paradigms, they make clear the norms and rules of acceptable and reasonable scholarship. From this point of view, any "good" scholar ought to be able to or should measure their scholarship by these paradigmatic "norms" to determine its credibility and legitimacy within the field of educational research. Identification within the paradigmatic hegemony as it is currently articulated allows legitimation of what is or is not important or reasonable—and sets up the boundaries for the inclusion or exclusion of those voices that do not conform or adhere to its norms, rules, and structures. However, given the omnipresence of racism, sexism, and cultural denigration that many African American and other scholars of color continue to face in the academy, the deeper meanings and possibilities of "paradigm proliferation" have profound implications for the process and presentation of our selves and our work in educational research. Those implications are taken up in the following section.

Paradigm Proliferation versus Possibilities: Power, Politics, and Paradox That's "Coloring" the Talk

If we hold that a paradigm is the articulation of the ways that scholars make sense of the research world they live in (and thus, the ways that we also make claims of legitimacy within and beyond our work), then the issue at hand seems *not* to be one of proliferation of paradigms. What is supremely at issue is that the articulation of what appears to be new productions of knowledge and new paradigms are as Richardson (1994) suggests "[hitting] us where we live—in our work and in our bodies" (p. 524). And because we are engaged in this discussion of proliferation at a time when there are increasing numbers of scholars of color who are articulating this "newness" is not coincidental but essential in recognizing the interplay of power and politics that is too often unarticulated in our discussions of research paradigms. But this interplay must be raised up: We must understand the complex ways that worldview, cultural knowledge, and identity are critical in the construction of any paradigm.

It is essential too that we examine the underlying knowledge of worldview, as worldview is always an essential part of the problem—and maybe the solution—to the questions put forth at the beginning of this chapter. What determines a scholar's worldview? Several scholars

(Dillard, 2000; hooks, 2000; Richards, 1980) have suggested that one of the most important factors is *cultural:* Our worldviews arise out of what those around us believe, our experience within the communities in which we live, and what those who are perceived as legitimate and powerful in our eyes tell us of the nature of the world. So we can say that the Big Four paradigms are cultural constructions which have arisen out of a broader research community, sanctioned by those who, by design or by default, have been perceived as legitimate and powerful, given the criteria of our profession (i.e., the number of research articles published, the perceived "quality" of scholarship, proliferation, and recognition of certain scholar's names, in other words, "stardom" as legitimacy, etc). From this standpoint, being able to talk about self as scholar and the worldview that grounds one's scholarship about one's scholarship location in terms of a recognized paradigm might feel like you do when plopping down in your favorite overstuffed chair after a long day's work: It makes you feel comfortable, rested, *at home*. Those who would argue that there is a problem in paradigm proliferation find it difficult to consider such proliferation as a moment of possibility, an inclusionary moment, a moment not just to feel comfortable in your own chair, but to pull up more chairs. Instead, many choose to themselves remain comfortably seated in the Big Four to avoid "suffering the death of cherished notions" (Peck, 1978, p. 193).

But here's the deal. The cherished notions of the Big Four paradigms often lie in a different direction than many African-centered scholars wish to travel, given the political and cultural nature of their construction. You see, contrary to popular belief, Black scholars are not white scholars who happen to be Black: We have fundamentally different ways of seeing and thinking about the world, what many White scholar colleagues may feel is a "violation" of prescribed ways of being, thinking, and representating, a violation at both the paradigmatic and epistemological levels (Dillard, 2000). As more and more African-ascendant scholars are immersing ourselves in cultural and spiritual spaces that are congruent with what we know (in body, mind, and spirit), we are also constructing more informed and authentic paradigms for ourselves, paradigms that allow us to emerge from and necessarily transgress the boundaries and norms of conventional social science. However, in our transgression (and unlike the reified Big Four), we make no claim to universal truth or appeal to others for membership or "protection." Like the story of the blind mice who touch parts of an elephant, each claiming they know the nature of the whole beast (Young, 1992), the critique of paradigm proliferation suggests to me that the fields of educational research and scholars' locations in their representative paradigms are struggling spiritually and intellectually with their own inadequacies, threatened by the unfamiliar Black scholar whose presence and thought challenges the very notions of what's held dear within the fields. Thus, at its very center, the often unnamed paradox for African-centered scholarship is a powerful and fundamental truth that just begs to be spoken—and which also powerfully undergirds the whole discussion of paradigm proliferation. This paradox is beautifully albeit painfully articulated in a poignant passage from an essay by James Baldwin (1988) titled "A talk to teachers":

> I decided very early that some mistake had been made somewhere. I was not a "nigger" even though you called me one. But if I was a "nigger" in your eyes, there was something about *you*—there was something *you* needed. I had to realize when I was very young that I was none of those things I was told I was. I was not, for example, happy. I never touched a watermelon for all kinds of reasons that had been invented by white people, and I knew enough about life by this time to understand that whatever you invent, whatever you project, is you! So where we are now is that a whole country of people believe I'm a "nigger," and I *don't*, and the battle's on! Because if I am not what I've been told I am, then it means that *you're* not what you thought *you* were *either!* And that is the crisis. (emphasis in original, p. 8)

So it's not really the proliferation of paradigms that is upsetting the research community. It's that the proliferation colors the talk in such a way that it upsets the notion of paradigms as an identity location, primarily for white scholars. What has passed for paradigmatic identity is a series of universalized stories (maybe even myths) about the goodness of particular paradigmatic notions. But this very postmodern critical moment, however, is also a cultural and spiritual one, holding important possibilities. In raising the very question of paradigm proliferation, we have at least begun to question the very meaning and hegemonic positions guiding our work as teachers and educational researchers. And, from my perspective, the path to living *within* the proliferation—and actually engaging in respectful and useful cross-paradigm dialogues—lies in letting go of the need to legitimate our work via a legitimating body (i.e., the Big Four). Instead, we must recognize the omnipresent ways that *every* researcher positions self as knower and teller of research stories. Such a notion inherently holds the assumption *that there is and will always be* as much paradigm proliferation as there are new and interesting people engaging in educational research. You see, it's not that, as a Black scholar, I can't locate my self/scholarship in the Big Four paradigms. I can, given that I was "trained" and socialized in the same institutions as many of my white scholar colleagues. But it's like buying a new pair of shoes. I usually wear a size 12. Now, I can squeeze my big feet into a size 11: I can actually "fit" inside the boundaries of the shoe. But it is very painful, terribly uncomfortable, and it is fundamentally too darn small! Should I continue to wear such a shoe, replete with the pain that would be the result for my whole body? And, at the place where many African-centered scholars have arrived today, we believe the smarter thing for us to do is to take the shoes back to the store and get some that fit, that we can wear comfortably. It's not that we don't find the knowledge that's been constructed into reified paradigms by other scholars as useful or important: We often do. Many of us just don't worship the Big Four or find any sort of solace within them. My solace is found in embracing a paradigm that arises from a worldview that is personal and cultural, a unique combination of what it means to be alive, as an African American woman scholar who is deeply attuned to the spiritual nature of my life and work.

"Subvert the Dominant Paradigm" or Embrace Your Own?: Exploring Issues of Spirit, Culture, and Race in Educational Research

I was visiting my parents in Seattle, Washington, when a 1960s Volkswagon Bug drove past me. On the back of the car was a very familiar bumper sticker, one that has always resonated with my spirit and made me smile. It says: "Subvert the dominant paradigm." However, on that day, it also encouraged me, reminding me to of the need to live out of an African-centered female sensibility and epistemological space in my life and work. For many African American women scholars, such resistant stances are truly appreciated and particularly helped us through our initial years as new teachers/scholars. However, as I write this chapter some 10 years later, I find myself much less interested in subverting the dominant paradigm than I am in embracing a dominant paradigm *of my own*. A paradigm that holds and embraces a version of truth that resonates with my very spirit and provides some congruence and support for the work that I do, as an African American woman scholar. Rather than subvert the Big Four (or worst yet, create a replicated "sub-version" of the same), I seek to embrace and create a paradigm that embodies and articulates a coherent sense of life around me, as an African American woman, one that can "tell them [in this case, the research community] what is important, legitimate and reasonable" (Patton, 1980, as cited in Donmoyer, 1999). One of the greatest implications for resistance and transformation of the sites and structures of our research and teaching endeavors is the possibilities of reframing research as a healing process, as a process of being of service in political and social change on behalf of the communities that one represents and is responsible to. From my perspective, such service is also a crucial and legitimate purpose for research. And maybe that is the reason for a paradigmatic stance: To be able to live and work within a space that resonates spiritually, culturally, and intellectually with one's work, regardless of issues of "proliferation." The next section discusses such a space.

Paradigms of the Spirit: Frameworks for the Political Work of Research and Teaching

"Only when spirit is at the center of our work can we create a community in love." This was an insight I wrote in my journal one morning during writing meditation. Writing is a daily spiritual practice for me, one that I have been committed to for nearly thirty years. But daily journal writing is also a spiritual practice that many of my academic peers and colleagues do not know exists in my life—and in the lives of other women as well. Along with prayer and meditation, it is a basis for a sort of spiritual awareness that Richards (1980) suggests helps us to make sense of our surroundings and to make sense of life and the universe—and the university! But among my colleagues, it seems much more "progressive" to speak about their distrust of things spiritual rather than to speak of devotion to a spiritual path. While I am committed to the notion of people doing their own thing, such distrust does renders a meaningful conversation about spirituality silenced and mostly unwelcomed in the everyday interactions in the university setting and marked as illegitimate in our scholarly discussions. And one of the strongest tensions that exists in choosing to place spirit at the center of academic work is that most of us don't want others to feel that, through the passion of our own beliefs and actions, we are trying to convert them or impose ideas about the power of the spirit on them.

But lately, I have begun to speak more openly about the central and sacred place of spirituality in my life, most often in response to the confusion and hopelessness of my students as they wrestle with the complexity of issues of difference and particularly multiculturalism in teaching and research (hooks, 1994). Like hooks, I find that many are angry that they've been denied certain histories (or more often herstories), having been educated through predominately white-, male-, and European-focused canons. Many are without hope, as they struggle to "do the right thing" in their own academic lives and find that their good intentions are a poor substitute for the cultural and experiential knowledge that they know they need but don't know how to get. Many are searching for ways to fill their rather empty hearts, having harbored lives full of abuse, neglect, and unloving family situations. Believing that it was their personal burden to bear these stories in silence, many have never dared to even utter them. Worse yet, many have never been *invited* to utter such stories, to speak their truths, especially in any place that resembled a school, not to mention in endeavors called research or teaching.

One of the ways I invite stories of the inner life into my graduate classes is to write weekly journals with my students. I engage in this practice as a way to model a more dialogic and pedagogically sound way of opening spaces for true sharing and being with one another and to open a space for students to begin to construct their own paradigms, to examine their own worldviews and their origins. And from my own experience in writing as spiritual practice, I've learned, as Julia Cameron (1999) has, that *writing rights things* (p. xiii). It can be a healing process. While topics for the our journals are self-chosen and thus vary widely throughout the quarter, I continue to be struck by how often the topics have included the necessity of love as a guiding principle for teaching, learning, and research, the role of courage as a researcher, and the struggles and oppression that often come to people of color and conscience in our academic lives as we explore and unpack the slippery notions of race, racism, and culture. What I've also learned is that, as I invite students to share such intimate and personal stories, it seems almost inhumane to just sit and listen without sharing my own experiences in dealing with similar issues in my own academic life. In creating spaces that are openly spiritual, *reciprocity is key:* Our desire is to know how we've become the persons we are meeting at that time. More particularly, my students want to know how I sustain my joy and recognize the purpose of my earthly journey, despite the pain and oppression that is often met by African American women academics and administrators within the walls of the academy. They want to know how to shape a life that sees the whole world as their community when so often the experiences of their lives barely reaches outside the small towns of their birth in any meaningful way. The most pressing concerns and questions that these future teachers and researchers pose are not *academic* questions: Their most pressing paradigmatic questions are about creating and engaging an academic life that is at the same time a spiritual life. They want to talk about how spirit is woven into our lives in divine ways that guide us, nourish us, and sustain us as human beings who have chosen the important work of teaching and research. Yes, the official content of the course explores multicultural education. But the *essential* content of the course explores our inner lives as teachers and researchers. And the power of the pedagogy can be heard in a note that Stacy, one of my students, wrote at the end of the course:

> You are the sun. I don't think I've ever met someone who radiates all good things as she enters a room. Your ideals, your vision, your capacity to share personal and profoundly sad pieces with your students is amazing. As I have expressed in journals, your lack of ego is a welcome gift for everyone who comes in contact with you . . . If ever I had a new shero, it is you. Thank you . . . for following your heart.

Stacy's voice—and countless others embodied in that voice—have been a catalyst for envisioning and transforming a different type of academic life, that is, to construct a view of teaching, research, and service within an openly spiritual paradigm. And fundamentally, such transformation comes from recognizing that being spiritual and centering spirituality is indeed *a legitimate way to participate in the social struggles of the world*. It comes from recognizing as hooks (2001) does that any effort we make to bring about peace and justice are indeed forms of spiritual practice.

Defining Spirituality

Speaking of a spiritual life and defining spirituality is fraught with difficulty. This is especially true when it comes to speaking of places and spaces that we've traditionally thought of as "academic." Like many folk who were educated in institutions of higher education, my academic beginnings were filled with a yearning to become an excellent student of the mind, a student who gave precious little time to spiritual activities like prayer, and singing and testifying. And in my quests for higher education, I came to understand that belief in something that is as invisible and unprovable as "the spirit" could have very dangerous consequences, especially to an academic career. Thus, I decided that the more "legitimate" way to define myself as an intellectual, especially as an African American woman, was to embrace an identity that allowed access and validation (albeit very limited) to white folks' academic circles. But as Wade-Gayles (1995) suggests about her own academic life (and I would painfully come to find out a bit later in my own),

> Such thinking, such behavior, such a belief system . . . is out of [seeking] consonance with white-male Western thinking which not only teaches dualism of the body and soul, but also elevation of the body *over* the soul. In a sense, then, I sought validation at the cost of my own soul. (p. 3, emphasis mine)

This is the dilemma often faced by African American women academics: How to embrace the resonances of our souls that arise from a spirituality that is the very fabric of Black life as we know it—and how to do so within academic contexts that have little energy for the spiritual, especially as expressed by an African American woman.

So, this discussion is about naming spirituality, about the power that is available to an academic life when one chooses to nourish the spirit within. It is about understanding that what we have all too often attributed to luck or coincidence or our own ability belongs to the workings of spirit. It is both about the process of transformation of our early "academic" perceptions and about moving spirituality from the margin of an academic life (and its paradigms) to the center. Finally, it is about putting forth such ideas for the considerations of others.

In many ways, the all encompassing nature of spirit and spirituality defies definition: *It is all that is.* However, in order to explore both its power and its influences in/on an academic life, we might begin to define spirituality not so much in terms of religious ideals, but as Hull (2001) does in her powerful book *Soul talk: The new spirituality of African American women:*

> Spirituality . . . involves conscious relationship with the realm of the spirit, with the invisibly permeating, ultimately positive, divine, and evolutionary energies that give rise to and sustain all that exists. (p. 2)

The key in this definition is that spirituality involves *consciousness.* It involves choosing to be in a relationship with the divine power of all things. And using this definition of spirituality, we can see being spiritual as a legitimate frame from and through which to participate in the social and political struggles of the world, including those we engage as academics. But, what then is the purposes of an academic life from such a standpoint and how might it be engaged? When the paradigm is reframed with body, mind, and spirit at the center, what we can engage as an academic life is transformed in significant ways.

First, *an academic life becomes a way and means to both serve humanity and to become more fully human in the process.* All of life is one life from a spiritual perspective. Thus, the separations we tend to make—between self and others, between students and professors, between researcher and researched—are false ones: From a spiritual standpoint, we are all one spirit, connected by the Creator's energy of breath. And as spirit, we are engaging in a human journey for as long as we have the energy of breath: When it is no longer ours, the human journey ends. But our spiritual essence continues its work, in a different realm, unencumbered by the body. While some refer to this as the ultimate freedom, I want to speak here of freedom in a slightly different way, in a way that is directly connected to the human journey of spirit that we are living right now and its relation to an academic life. My ideas about freedom are greatly influenced by Brazilian educator and thinker Paulo Freire (1970) who says that

<blockquote>
Freedom is acquired by conquest not by gift. It must be pursued constantly and responsibly. Freedom is not an ideal located outside of man; nor is it an idea which becomes a myth. It is rather the indispensable condition for the quest of human completion. (p. 31)
</blockquote>

In other words, becoming fully human is the very work of being human. This can be seen as an echo of Du Bois's spiritual striving: About becoming more humane, more kind, more loving as human beings in relationship with one another and with all of life. I would like to suggest here that a paradigm surrounding research and teaching that is consciously engaged toward freedom of body, mind, and spirit of all involved, can be framed with service to humanity as its goal. And such service begins with engaging oneself, as the researcher or teacher, in continuous reflection, examination, and exploration of one's heart and mind for the true purposes of one's work. In this way, research and teaching are not just something you do, but something you are engaged *with*, a way of being in the world in relationship with others. Fundamentally, if we see research and teaching as both intellectual *and* spiritual endeavors, then the purpose of our research will be to more fully love and serve human beings and to serve life. In this way, the academic life of a teacher or researcher will not be centered in the long-standing, ego driven rewards we've held up in the academy as important, but instead on making the world a better place, on ending oppression, on becoming more fully human ourselves through the work that we do in the world.

Second, *an academic life is creative and seeks to heal mind, body, and spirit*. Human beings are creations. As human beings, we are meant to continue being creative, as the divine Creator's force extends through us, manifesting the dreams of the universe through the work that we do. Such creativity should be central to the purpose of research and teaching. Teaching and research practices are dynamic and creative practices, not solely practices of the mind: Engaging one's spirit as a part of those practices is key to the creation and transformation of one's inner and outer life—and thus, the whole of life. But I am reminded by the voice of Audre Lorde (1984) when she states that

<blockquote>
my fullest concentration of energy is available to me only when I integrate all the parts of who I am, openly, allowing power from particular sources of my living to flow back and forth freely through all my
</blockquote>

different selves, without the restrictions of externally imposed definition. (pp. 120–121)

She is suggesting that when we acknowledge and embrace such a creative spirituality in teaching and research, it must encompass the whole of one's human-ness: It must help us to reconcile and re-member mind, body, and spirit as we engage our work. It must help us to deal with our intentions in our interactions and dealings with one another, creating new possibilities to address the myriad of social and economic issues that are the current contexts for our research and teaching. *A course in miracles* (1975) tells us that what we perceive as differences and separations between us (such as race, ethnicity, na-tion, gender, geography, language, and culture) are but illusions from a spiritual perspective (this is taken up more fully in Chapter 7). It must help us to see time—and our relation to time as human beings—as part of the same past, present, and future.

Finally, *an academic life is a political life, with peace and justice as its aim.* It is a life that arises from a paradigm that values the recog-nition of politics as an embodied and embedded catalyst and guide for our teaching and research endeavors. As I suggested in the tenets of an endarkened feminist epistemology in Chapter 1, all that we do in every aspect of our lives speaks volumes about what we value and believe to be true about whatever we are undertaking, whether teach-ing, research, or service. We acknowledge by our every action, whether peace and justice are fundamental to the well-being of human rela-tionships and life on this planet. From my perspective, this is not an optional part of an academic life that places spirit at the center. Part of our responsibility as teachers and researchers is to engage in con-tinual examination, reflection, and definition of who we are in our academic lives—and who we are becoming. This will give us insight into ways to create an academic life that serves and does not destroy and that resists those spaces and places that resist social justice, through embracing a paradigm where culture and spirit are central and peace and justice is the work.

A Telling Postscript: How I Came to This Paradigm Project

Seldom do we tell the genesis of our projects, that is, the path that brings us to a particular project at a particular time. And often, such a journey is even more illustrative than the "official" narratives that we tell, the data stories of our research. As a person of African ascent, the journey also points out the often paradoxical work of being both a *living thinker* (James, 1993) and one who inhabits a Black women's body, in continual pursuit of ways of being that are African centered and spiritually resonant.

I remember the day when my colleague and friend called and invited me to be a part of the American Educational Research Association (AERA) session that she and another colleague were proposing—and that was the genesis of my early thoughts and writings about the subject of paradigms. As she explained the history of the project, I saw the catalyst for the session came out of a published space that I was personally intrigued with, that is, the relationship between paradigm proliferation and the notion of coloring epistemologies (Scheurich & Young, 1997). I listened excitedly to the invitation my colleague friend put forth. But my heart dropped as I heard her proposition: "We'd like you to be a discussant for our papers (along with Handel Wright, another researcher of African ascent). While very interested in the topic, I objected and strongly resisted the subject position and role that I'd been placed in. If there had been cartoon balloons above my head, the monologue would have gone something like this: "Oh, no they didn't, not again. It's not even *possible* for them to consider researchers of color as a part of the *main* discussion! They have to cast the only two Black folk who've been invited to the party as discussants of *their* ideas about the writing and thinking of folk of color . . ." I could feel myself calming down. "Okay, the invitation is coming from good friends and colleagues. But right now, I am all too weary of 'coloring' the commentary, of being the postscript, of validating and legitimizing liberal white voices . . ." So, I countered the invitation: I'd be willing to participate not as a discussant, but as one of the main paper presenters. And I'd examine (and enact in a subject-to-subject way), the troubling state of the paradigm talk and coloring epistemologies discussion, one that has been constructed largely by white researchers objectifying folks of color without a concomitant discussion *with us*.

So this postscript describing the journey to this project is also a story of bearing witness to the larger overt and covert conversations on coloring epistemologies and paradigm proliferation. Frankly? It was in good measure plain old irritation and an ongoing pursuit of social justice that fueled my response and decision to engage in the discussion. But, in return, what I received was the benefit of the critique and healing that always comes when folks of color speak for ourselves and in our own voices.

Much of that healing came through what Patti Lather calls the "firestorm of publication," those lessons I'd also learned in having spent more than five years attempting to actually be a *published* participant in the "lively discussion" that Scheurich and Young called for in their initial paper on coloring epistemologies, the actual impetus for this discussion on paradigm proliferation. While all scholars feel the sting of publication rejection letters, scholars of color whose scholarship embraces life as we understand and live it, all too often also experience a very vicious process of censorship and gatekeeping, with its underlying basis in racism, sexism, and other forms of exclusion. But unlike other rejections that had come when I write research in more conventional representative ways and about more general multicultural education or pedagogical practices, I've learned that the gatekeepers are more vigilant, ruthless, and even violent when an African-ascendant scholar calls into question the very nature of knowledge and its constituent representations. So the opportunity for a public forum like that AERA session provided at least a small segment of the academic community access to the ideas was a critical one (9).

But this AERA session was also important on several substantive levels, relative to our focus on spirit and culture in an academic life. First, it provided a way to present and explore contexts for unpacking the political, personal, and spiritual nature of paradigm talk and research endeavors. Handel Wright's ability to raise intriguing questions that challenged and engaged the deeper meanings and tensions of proliferation (and the often masked or ignored cultural, social, racial, gendered nature of paradigm talk) was brilliant and lead to a provocative follow-up publication of response and response to the response for both of us (see Wright, 2003 and Dillard, 2003, for the follow-up theorizing between us). While I found some agreement across the three presented papers about the nature of paradigm proliferation, this agreement existed as both a space of tension and possibility. Fundamentally, unlike my colleagues, I see all talk (including paradigm

talk) as always political and in all ways raced, a deeply cultural endeavor that embodies both the intellect and the spirit. For many
African American women scholars, talk is *productive* to the extent
that we can think and feel with it *as African American women* scholars
and bring its words to bear in the service of purposes and problems
greater than ourselves. Thus, my intent in talking about paradigms
was to disrupt the talk and enliven action as fundamental to what it
means to engage in research as a reciprocal relationship between and
among human beings and toward a social justice aim.

Second, in terms of possibilities of paradigm talk and coloring
epistemologies, my resonance in the session was with Handel's very
careful discussion of our work. From an endarkened epistemological
space, one can only read productively when one has the cultural
knowledge to make meaning of the text (Appiah, 1992). For the first
time in my academic career, I actually heard and felt someone engage
that sort of reading of the text, at a level of intellectual and spiritual
understanding. But it was the reverent, caring, and humane way that
Handel simultaneously critiqued and affirmed the work that provided
me new ways to consider the usefulness—and the problematics—of an
endarkened feminist epistemology as a tool within and against the
coloring epistemologies and paradigm talk.

My research and teaching interests lie in rethinking critical
theory/pedagogies and multicultural teacher education. But as Parker
Palmer (1993) suggests, fundamental shifts are needed at the level of
epistemology, in how we know and the nature of knowledge itself. As
we are cultural beings, knowledge is also a culturally constructed
commodity. Thus, we must continue to explore and uncover those
epistemological spaces where the deeply cultured and spiritual realities of those who may find little resonance with the reified paradigms
in educational research exist might "endarken" and/or otherwise transform what we have come to believe to be our rather "enlightened"
paradigms in contemporary educational research and teaching.

3

Walking Ourselves Back Home

The Education of Teachers With/In the World

Introduction: I Am Here in the World

I am here in the world
and the world is here in me,
each breath
a reminder to me of
the connections that sustain
the very substance of life,
of people . . .

I am here in Ten Sleep, Wyoming. . . .
on a Girl Scout trip
designed for underprivileged, inner city,
girls of color.
All dressed in shiny new
Girl Scout "gear,"
I kissed my mother and father good-bye
and climbed through the doors of the van,
on the first of many journeys
that would open my eyes
to a world
beyond Seattle, Washington,
beyond this colored girl's sense of time,
beyond this colored girl's sense of space.
I would see Glacier National Park
with trees so tall I couldn't see their tops,

and Old Faithful, with all of its sulphur and spit.
I would ride Charro, my palamino pony
and get a tick that scared me to death.
I would dig for arrow heads
and realize the ways of ancient people's.
I would watch sun set pink and orange
over the terra-cotta Rockies.
Most of all,
I would ride on a plane
and realize how vast and wide these
United States are
and how those little lines
we called borders in U.S. history
did not really exist
from the window of a plane. . . .

I am here in Britain . . .
my first trip
"overseas,"
I learned that
I didn't like smashed peas
but I loved drinking beer in the pubs
and ploughman's lunches.
That castles are real
and going to the markets
was a social event for women,
as long as you had a good wicker basket
and a story to tell.
That green is so green on the hills of Scotland
and that heather is both a color and a flower,
as peaceful as it is breathtaking.
As I sat night after night with the innkeepers
over tea and biscuits and a smoky fire,
We talked of politics, and race,
and who's English was the "real thing,"
And I learned that teachers are everywhere
if you are open to the lessons they have to teach you . . .

I am here in Mexico. . . .
not a lick of Spanish to my name,
but my boyfriend and I
had dreamed of this trip

and, even though he was now gone,
my dream remained
and so did my determination. . . .
I cried a lot on this first trip sur de la frontera,
But each time a tear fell,
an angel appeared to make it bien,
the guy who showed me the right bus to San Miguel de Allende,
the teacher at my school who would make me speak Spanish:
"Cynthia, cómo se llama este cosa¿"
"Cynthia, dónde esta la mesa (or the door or the store or whatever)¿
I personally think that she just liked the name Cynthia,
I'm really not sure she liked me.
I for sure despised this woman then,
but I adore her now,
Because humility is always good
for a person with lots of "education,"
Because empathy for the difficulty of learning a language can only truly
be known through experiences,
Because the passion that I now have for language—all language
and the ways in which it opens the world to you
and you to the world,
I'll never forget. . . .

I am here in El Salvador,
my politics urging me south
to understand the deeper meanings
of concepts I throw around carelessly
like war and poverty
peace and prosperity
like developed and underdeveloped
like Third World and First World
like faith and hope
like responsibility and solidarity.
I lived within a comunidad
which many would say was poor
But
as I listened to the U.S.-supplied bombs fall like rain,
as I ate my beans and tortillas and listened to stories of everyday life,
as I talked with the children and heard them sing their revolutionary songs,
as I knelt in the dirt with everyone else for fourteen stations of the cross,
I learned
That being poor materially does not mean being poor spiritually:

I was amongst some of the richest people I had ever met,
That countries are intimately connected and
That their relationship should be reciprocal and respectful.
That faith, as I had practiced it
could be a part-time thing,
when hard times came or when I might find the time.
Los Salvadorenos reminded me that real faith
is a full-time commitment based on the premise
that today is all you have, and
tomorrow is never promised.

I am here in Switzerland, Germany, France, and the Netherlands,
where the Alps dwarf me,
where wine and good friends are the standard,
where sailing became a pasttime,
and
I am here in Japan, where I learned the difference between private
    and public,
and the power of presentation
and
I am here in Hong Kong, I am here in Pakistan, where I helped to open
    a school
and
I am here in Thailand, where I taught teachers about diversity and how
    education can acknowledge culture in all of its complexity,
and

I have always been here in Africa,
but now I know
from having walked Her earth
over and over again,
I know
way deep down inside my bones,
the place where the strength
of the African American comes
and
I can see
what I am and
who I am
and I can live in that space
for the rest of my life,
breathing fully,

the grace of a past world
that guides me
in this world and
let's me know
that the world
is at home
right here
in me.

I wrote this poem in 1998. I look back on it now as a piece that embodied my notions of what teaching, learning, and living were at that time—and to some extent, even now. It was written in a graduate course on multicultural education, the outcome of an assignment where both my students and I reflected on what we considered the multicultural influences in our lives and then shared those insights in creative ways within our graduate classroom community. And while I revel in being creative, I realize in reflection, that one of my assumptions in giving this assignment to my students was that, as educators, we can best learn about our selves by reflecting on our lives *alone*. In the stillness of our own thoughts. In solo spaces. That the lessons of our lives are embodied in who we believe ourselves to be. Now certainly my own teaching life and perspectives about multicultural and international education have been radically transformed through deep self-awareness and introspection on my own motivations, desires, and the practice that follow from them. I believe this is a fundamental truth for all who educate and will be taken up throughout this chapter. But the profound realization that prompted this writing is not so much that I had been wrong all of these years in caring about and engaging in self-reflection as a critical part of education: It is that self-reflection was and is not enough to sustain our lives and roles as educators if our purpose is to powerfully engage the minds, bodies, and spirits of the diverse students we teach and are taught by. In addition to self-reflection, we must engage the power that transcends what I can now see through this poem is the illusion of my reflection as somehow being all about me. Solely and totally separate, albeit in and of the world, interestingly nuanced through my own private difference, of and for myself alone. Today, I am suggesting that our human diversity is our strength and that we are already unified by two truths more powerful than our individual stories. The first truth is that as people of earth, we are unified through breath. Intimately and absolutely connected. The second truth is that each one of us is spirit. The embodied energy of life. These are the fundamental truths that unify us as human beings and as teachers and researchers. It is about understanding that our unity with others—whether our students, colleagues, society, the world—is influenced deeply by the ways in which we are in unity with ourselves and the ways in which we re-member spirit in education in our unity with others.

I reflect on the following passage from Ghanaian author Ayi Kwei Armah's book *Two thousand seasons:*

> The teachers told us quietly that the way of experts had become a tricky way. They told us it would always be fatal to our arts to misuse the skills we had learned. The skills themselves were mere light shells, needing to be filled out with substance coming from our souls. They warned us never to turn these skills to the service of things separate from the way . . . Our way, the way, is not a random path. Our way begins from coherent understanding. It is a way that aims at preserving knowledge of who we are, knowledge of the best way we have found to relate each to each, each to all, ourselves to other peoples, all to our surroundings. If our individual lives have a worthwhile aim, that aim should be a purpose inseparable from the way . . . Our way is reciprocity. The way is wholeness. (Armah, 1973, p. 39)

Armah's last line "the way is wholeness," suggests that integrity is an important notion in articulating the spiritual nature of our academic lives. Soundness, completeness, unity of mind, body, and spirit. But it also suggests something that is often missing in the call for self-reflection and unity within our lives as educators who truly teach with and in the world: That missing element is the need to engage the *experiences* that unite us. The abundance of literature on research and teaching suggests that we know much about their techniques, curriculum, methodology, and the like. But how often do we pause to consider the deeper guidance and energies of our working lives in concert with others? The reasons and purposes for what we do? Whether a sense of integrity manifests in our lives as researchers and teachers? This is the task taken up here, with two central questions as the mission of this chapter: What knowledge about teaching and research might we glean from an openly spiritual educator who is deeply influenced through community and experiences "in the world," most specifically in the

United States and in Ghana, West Africa? Further, how might such knowledge provide ways to reflect on and to ground our own selves and our work in teacher education, in community with others?

You must know that this piece arises out of my own desire, as an educator of over twenty years, to reflect deeply on my teaching and research and the lives and experiences of other African ascendent teachers in a sort of wholeness—culturally, relationally, spiritually, and in community with others. It is not by accident that I focus my attention, as an African ascendent educator, on my experiences in and of Ghana, West Africa. For most African ascendents who have been raised here in the United States, our definitions and identity, however powerful, have been developed against the backdrop of insidious racism, sexism, classism, and other "ism's" that, by their very nature, are limiting, always about who we are *not* versus about who we *are*. These are also not empowering realities: They are realities that move us further away from following the way that Armah suggested, further away from unity of humans through breath and spirit. As my interest in the spiritual nature of education has grown in my own life and more explicitly in my practices as an educator, I began to ask deeper questions of my own identity, my connections to others through my purpose, which is teaching: What would happen to my life, my teaching and research practice if I were to immerse myself even more deeply in that which is African, both as a way of being and as a way of thinking? How does living and being in day-to-day experiences with others in Ghana as an African ascendent raised in the United States influence one's perspectives not only about what it means to be an African ascendent, but about how one is a spiritually engaged teacher in unity or community with others? Finally, what is my purpose as an African ascendent and how do I "be" in community with something greater than myself that at the same time honors the communities in which I work and live as an educator and researcher?

The hardest part of this journey has been to love these questions, to honor myself enough not to search for the answers, but instead to live everything, to gradually live my way into the answers, as Rilke (1934) says. It has not been easy, and certainly, all my questions have not yet been answered! In many ways, this is a very particular story of one African ascendent teacher's journey and the ways that spiritual integrity—connections of mind, body, and spirit—have been "uncovered" within my life and teaching work through my

experiences in Ghana particularly and the world generally. The thesis
here is that these connections would have been unavailable except
through the real *experiences* of sitting still in meditation or delightedly
sharing a cold beer on the shores of Cape Coast or fiercely debating
issues of identity and cultural politics between Africans living on the
continent and as an African living in the Americas. These experiences have certainly made me even more aware of who I am, whose
I am, and of my life as a teacher, leader and a researcher. However
even more important, I am hoping that others might seek to engage
direct experiences within their own communities of care and connection and that these might be seen as central goals of teacher education
"of the spirit," created primarily through the very acts of engaging self
and others *within* the intimacy and vulnerability that living as spirit
(versus solely as body) require. And in examining more deeply an example of African/African American lived pedagogy in international
contexts, we can attune to the deeper spiritual reservoirs within those
experiences and draw from them lessons of teaching, learning, and
living that can profoundly inform—and transform—our work *together*.
And the more stories we uncover, from such multiple cultural spaces,
the more able we might be to foster a balance of the spiritual, emotional, and intellectual development of ourselves and our students in
today's culturally diverse settings. Palmer (1983) suggests that such
aims could represent an authentic spirituality in education that

> wants to open us to truth, whatever truth may be, wherever truth
> might take us. Such a spirituality does not dictate where we must go,
> but trusts that any path walked with integrity will take us to a place
> of knowledge. (p. xi)

There are five key notions for the reader to bear in mind throughout this chapter about the nature of spiritually centered education,
especially for teachers. First, spiritual education is at once a personal
and social endeavor, engaged through one's self and others. Second,
education that attends to the spiritual is intimate, connected, and
often requires us to be vulnerable, to re-member our collective humanity. Third, education that is spiritual arises from engaging *experiences* between and among our diverse ways of being and knowing.
Fourth, spiritual education and the teaching that follows from it requires that a sense of integrity manifest in our lives and roles as

teachers. Integrity in this case refers to a conscious attention to unity of mind, body, and spirit of one's self and others. Finally, deeply listening to stories from diverse and multiple contexts and peoples of the world can ultimately influence and help to develop our competence and humility as multicultural teachers and researchers in/of the world. The next sections are examples of the beginnings of my own engagement with these five notions through my journey and experiences in Ghana, West Africa.

The Importance of Home

A few years ago, I had the opportunity to arrange a trip to Ghana for my elder sister, Mother, and two aunts. Since none had ever traveled to the continent of Africa before, I carefully arranged all of the details of the trip and accompanied them as well. Because of my extensive experience traveling, doing research, and teaching in Ghana, I was very comfortable in my role as "teacher-tour guide," their full expectations being that I embodied and carried expertise that would not only make everything run smoothly but would enhance their experience of Ghana. And part of that expectation was to help them to find *home* in Ghana, a somewhat mythical space that many African Americans yearn for in our pilgrimages to Africa, given our historical and contemporary oppressions and marginalizations as African "Americans." But, unbeknownst to me, the real power of this trip was in being able to observe and participate in their experiences of "homecoming" to Africa, to occupy together a space that was both transformative and healing to us all, as persons of African ascent. And in this experience, I was no longer solely teacher but also *taught*, catching glimpses of the critical and complicated dynamics of creating safe spaces that truly honor cross-cultural and international realities and identities. And homecoming serves as a fitting metaphor for the fundamental work of multicultural teacher education in the world, that is in helping teachers to understand (and often unpack) their own metaphorical "home" as a precursor to understanding the diverse settings in which they live and work in the world. A journal entry illustrates this best:

> *Coming home . . . It really is the case that I recognize so many places as home. Like the tortoise so revered here in Ghana, I carry my home with*

me . . . So the whole idea of my walking the elders back home really is about walking them—and myself—back to a place that is our center; a peaceful place where we can find respite, that is a safe haven for our bodies, minds, and spirits. A place that is a refuge, a homeplace and that is especially a space that can sustain us. These African lessons for us African wimmin elders were all about ourselves. About each of seeing and hearing and feeling our own way back home, guided by our collective experiences, of our every-day life here in Africa. Like Morrison's unspeakable unspoken, coming back to this home is about finding the familiar in the unfamiliar, about seeing and feeling things that are at the same time known and unknown: Known enough to be familiar and resonate with one's soul and at the same time strange enough that one yearns to understand, to know more, and to experience the depth of one's own soul . . . (Journal, 12/27/00)

As we engage in a search for the multiple truths that inevitably arise in teacher education that focuses on international and multicultural education and social justice, part of this search is about each one of us "walking ourselves back home." What I am suggesting here is that there are voices and texts, canons and conversations that we have not heard in teacher education and that are critical to pre-paring global education professionals.

I have chosen to describe this journey, I will again shift to life notes discourse (Bell-Scott, 1994). As mentioned in Chapter 1, life notes refer broadly to constructed personal narratives such as letters, stories, journal entries, reflections, poetry, music, and other artful forms of data. It is important to remember that life notes as data also carry deeper meanings when consciously attending to a whole academic life, embedded in sociocultural contexts and communities of affinity. An important assumption guiding my choice in this forum is that African diasporic voices and the "theory" contained in them, have not been broadly utilized in mainstream teacher education, even as they have been continually and constantly constructed and utilized within African American communities and contexts to give sense and meaning to one's life. Finally, and more specifically, I believe that African women's voices embodied in life notes can be seen as special-ized bodies of knowledge which, while legitimate and powerful, have been excluded from the stores of knowledge under girding most teacher education research, literature and practice. My hope through utilizing life notes to describe and explore my own experiences in Ghana is that you will experience this text as Bethel (1982) suggested earlier as an "overheard conversation" in addition to an actual literary text (p. 180).

My experience traveling with the elders was the catalyst for deeper thinking about the meaning of home, as I have attempted over these past few years to craft a home for myself as an educator on both sides of the water, that is, in Ghana and in the United States. But it was also the beginning of deeper thinking about the "home" that each of my preservice and inservice teachers brings to the classroom context that embodies (or doesn't) understandings of the world that allow them to truly teach all for whom they areresponsible.

The next section highlights the journey that has lead me to my current work in Ghana, which includes building (from the ground up!) and codirecting a preschool in the village of Mpeasem in the Central Region of Ghana. I have been honored in that work by being named Queen Mother of Development for the village, a position of honor that I will hold for the rest of my life (see Chapters 5 and 6 for specific discussions of this role and work). As I have found work in Ghana to be deeply spiritual work for everyone involved, I acknowledge that presence by using, as introductions, lines of a meditation I've written called *Building a School* (10). This meditation seeks to share the insights, revelations, and knowledge I continue to glean as a teacher and researcher, about the historical and cultural nature of Africa generally and Ghana more specifically. While sometimes unconscious to persons of African ascent living in the United States and the diaspora, I believe that these knowings still run through our veins and thus, manifest in our teaching and research, our academic lives. I use this meditation to further point to the tensions, contradictions, struggles, and joys that are *available* to all of us when we engage and work in culturally diverse or intercultural sites with spirituality as the centerpiece of our work. These experiences can indeed be powerful "classrooms" for transformation and growth as a human being and as a teacher.

Building a School: The Healing Wisdom of Mpeasem (11)
Mpeasem is a true testament to its name:
It means "We don't want any trouble."
We just want a school.
Gracious Creator,
I thank you for bringing me to this village!
A place where building the community through children is the project,

A place where parents love their kids
and know that education and opportunity
are intimately connected
To freedom . . .

My first trip to Ghana was in 1995, as part of a tour of educators from New York. And the minute the moist tropical air embraced me as I stepped out of the airplane, I knew it was a special place. My soul awakened in Africa! The first few years (and multiple trips) after the first were spent working on a qualitative research project focused on schools, community, and culture in Ghana, with special attention on the explicit connections between all three in the SOS Children's Village in Tema, a suburb of the bustling capital city of Accra.

While most of my travels had taken me to the interior of Ghana, in 1996, I taught a one-week multicultural course at the University of Cape Coast and began to establish relationships with the teacher education community there. However, the deeper establishment was my own enchantment with the Cape Coast and Elmina area, given its historical and cultural significance to African Americans. This was especially true in my visits to the slave dungeons that dot the sea coast there. In those dungeons, the cultural memories of the slave trade were alive in my body, as the ancestors spoke to me of the importance of my return to Ghana: I had come full circle, back to the place of my people.

I was introduced to the village of Mpeasem by a friend, Dr. Jemima Hayfron-Benjamin, a Ghanaian medical doctor who runs a small clinic in Elmina. Our friendship developed over time, characterized by lively discussions about her experience in medical school in Germany as a Ghanaian, and my experiences in Ghana as an African American. One day, she announced (without a chance for me to question): "I want to take you to a village that I think you'll really love." And so was my introduction to Mpeasem. A small village of about 300 people, it is as beautiful as it is rife with abject poverty. Situated in a big valley surrounded by shrub clad hills, the busy West African highway that connects Accra and the port city of Takoradi divides the village in two. I was immediately struck by the thatched-roof wattle and daub (mud) houses, the smiling farmers, women in the community washing clothes in big aluminum tubs, chickens and goats wandering wherever they pleased, and small smiling barefoot children who seemed to be everywhere! It was a beautiful sight, especially as my eyes met the smiling eyes of those who lived in Mpeasem.

One of the first things that attracted my attention as we walked to the village chief's palace was what looked like four corner pillars in the center of the village, some sort of beginnings of a building. When I inquired about its purpose, the Chief and the Elders explained that it had been the beginning of a town hall and school that could not be built because there was no money to do so. In my mind (or was that my heart?), I thought: As an educator, I believe deeply that education is a fundamental human right, one that should be available to all children regardless of the geographic location, nation state or condition of their birth. It was a critical moment for me: Was this a rhetorical principle in my teaching life or did I believe this to be true enough to take action right here in Mpeasem?

> *. . . I buy the materials.*
> *The women carry aluminum basins filled with rocks*
> *on their heads, their backs strong and straight.*
> *And the men mix cement,*
> *shovel dirt from the floor,*
> *measure boards for cutting against one another,*
> *with the accuracy that's found in the finest of tools.*
> *You said we will know a person by their work, Lord,*
> *And this work shows a community that is serious!*
> *I'm grateful for Your gift of Mpeasem,*
> *a chance to share the abundance that You've given me*
> *and to receive abundantly in ways I'd never imagined . . .*

I made the commitment: We would have a community center and preschool in the village of Mpeasem, to both serve the more than 60 children in the village who had no school to attend and to provide a town hall for the village. Several preliminary meetings were held with the Chief and Elder Council. We purchased supplies in town to begin the building and transported them to the site. And on Wednesday, November 3, 1999, the work began on the community center, amid an overwhelming reception! Sacred rituals such as pouring libations were done, special speeches and blessings were performed. And as a Queen Mother, I am now an integral part of such ceremonies and can more deeply appreciate their functions in maintaining community and connections between those who have died and "gone home," those who are here, and those who are to come.

Communal labor was engaged to do the work: I agreed to provide all the necessary financial assistance to complete the building and start the school. Throughout the next year, as I saved and shared, the building began to take shape. And in January 2001, I was there to witness the children of Mpeasem—my children—hold their first classes, with a teacher "on loan" from the village. It was indeed a happy day!

> *. . . I'm also grateful*
> *For Your life lessons*
> *About the meaning of giving*
> *Of service*
> *Of "Mpeasem,"*
> *Of learning to give unconditionally*
> *With no expectations of return,*
> *Of giving unselfishly*
> *Just for its own sake,*
> *And in the spirit of love . . .*

> *. . . Of learning to ignore the criticisms,*
> *Often heard from my*
> *African American brothers and sisters,*
> *Who, in fear of loss, urge me*
> *Not to trust the Ghanaians because*
> *"their motives are not honest:*
> *they sold us once and they'll do it again" . . .*

The road to building the community center was not always easy and required negotiations—and prayer—throughout the process. In reflection, there were several challenges that are worth noting for those interested in teaching and work cross-culturally. First, throughout the process of building the community center and school, I had to learn to trust my own instincts, intuition and intentions, as an African American. Historically, relations and understandings between Africa and the United States (and the African diaspora more generally) was severely undermined by the overwhelming horror of the enslavement of innocent African people, the subsequent brutalities of the Middle Passage, and the institution of slavery in the United States and throughout the world. Regardless of place of birth, the conditions of African people—emotionally, economically, spiritually, education-ally—have been deeply affected by this historical travesty. For me, this meant trying to listen carefully to everyone's needs, desire, and advice about the project—and following my own heart in the end.

A second challenge was an economic one, that is, prioritizing my own resources in such a way that we could finish the community center and school in a timely manner. And as Queen Mother, this responsibility is tied to a progressive development agenda for my vil-lage of Mpeasem, one that includes future fund-raising through devel-opment of a nonprofit charitable foundation.

The final challenge has to do with my role as a faculty member in multicultural teacher education at a large Midwestern research university. How could the preschool in Mpeasem, Ghana, provide reciprocal opportunities for cross-cultural/international teaching and learning experiences for the Mpeasem teachers as well as teachers from the United States? We are beginning now to have some discus-sions about the rich possibilities for teacher exchange and curriculum development, especially for those interested in the education of African-ascendant children.

> *. . . Father-Mother God,*
> *Building for children is so important*
> *In teaching us how to detach*
> *From the outcomes we desire*
> *And to attach to Your divine order and timing.*
> *Building this school*
> *Needed no control from me*
> *But it did need trust in Your able guidance,*
> *Of human hands, hearts, and minds*
> *Toward harmony and ultimately*
> *Toward good.*

> *Mostly Lord,*
> *I thank you for the lesson*
> *Of trust in my Self and my intentions,*
> *As a woman, a mother, an African and a teacher.*
> *I am more capable of right action*
> *Than I sometimes believe.*
> *And children deserve nothing less from us.*

The building of the school in Mpeasem lead Village Chief Nana Nyam IV and the Elders to honor my work in Mpeasem in two ways. The first is that the community center was named in my honor. The second is that on June 23, 2001, I was enstooled as Queen Mother Nana Mansa II of Mpeasem. For this special ceremony, I organized a tour group of 15 interested teachers, students, family, and friends to both witness and participate in this event. And as an educator, I know this work in Mpeasem is just the beginnings of a lifetime of spirited and healing work, work that continues to build bridges across continents, people, and traditions, to "re-member," to put it all back together, as part of education with/in the world.

Reflections on the Importance of International and Multicultural Sites of Practice and Service

Freire (1970) and hooks (1989) suggest that critical consciousness and broader perspectives are developed by coming face-to-face with contradictions in life that require a reexamination of values, cultural understandings, and decision-making—where what we hold dear and understand does not work or is not applicable. Through my own life experiences "in the world" I have found international experiences to be both critical and crucial sites of contradictions as well as important locations for transformation and reconstruction of my perspectives of teaching and learning. Although I've highlighted a very personal story of my own spiritual and cultural transformation, it is hoped that through engaging the personal, we can actually transform our own thinking, those perspectives that prohibit us from seeing diversity and international experiences as absolutely critical for the life and work of teachers and teacher educators.

So, what does all of this mean for learning and teaching education practices? At the risk of seeming simplistic, here are at least some of the ways in which our own praxis and practice can be changed and transformed through these experiences.

First, through in-depth international experiences, *we develop relationships in the world and a relationship with the world that more closely mirrors and affirms community* as I believe it needs to be understood or conceptualized: As connected, interrelated, whole, global. International experiences, given in-depth orientation and study, can indeed lead to moving past being a "tourist" or a visitor in unknown territory and in unfamiliar ways, to deeper more complex, spiritual meanings of teaching, culture, and the way toward more substantive human relationships.

Second, through international experiences, *we are better able to define and situate ourselves—and our students—in relationship to and within the diversity of humanity.* For example, as an African American critical feminist academic, my work in the world has moved me to push beyond my own stereotypic and exotic notions of the "other" to broader, more informed understandings of both the particular as well as the universal nature of African people—and my own place in those understandings. I have further been challenged to recognize my responsibility as an African-ascendant educator and as an African American feminist researcher to create connections on both sides of the water—and to attempt to live honorably in both spaces.

Third, *educating teachers in the world provide a plethora of opportunities to learn new symbol systems, languages, and dialects, and at least some partial understanding of the subtle and not-so-subtle cultural nuances with which to then teach and dialogue with folks within and outside of the United States.* It is always amazing—and useful—to be able to utilize familiar discourses with as many of our students as possible. So the more languages and dialects that we have available to use, the better. And I've found that even the most feeble attempts to dialogue in student's first language carry deep and important meanings that may need to be communicated, for students to feel "at home."

Fourth, *these experiences increase one's cultural knowledge.* We develop broader range of experiences, information, realia, and "texts" that we are able to bring to bear in our own teaching and learning that we did not previously possess.

Fifth, and finally, *there is a confidence and esteem in having thrived within international contexts.* For me, there is also a deep sense of humility that I inherently feel as I learn to depend on others to help me grow and adapt in places that are new and unfamiliar. And always, international contexts prove to be sites through which I can learn and theorize and develop a praxis of the world. As I attempt to interpret life around me, I am constantly reminded of the ways that I must "follow the talk I talk with the walk I walk." I invite you—all of you—to reflect on and engage in praxis responsive to the world as a community, a place that we *all* can call home.

4

Looking at the Real Nature of Things

Life and Death as One Eternal Moment
in Teaching and Research

> *Rid the world of philosophers and theorists.*
> *Throw out all the research studies.*
> *Then the importance of people will come to the fore . . .*
>
> —D. Smith, *The Tao of dying*

In considering the meanings of research and teaching as spiritual practice, I was lead to a book by Thich Nhat Hanh and Daniel Berrigan titled *The raft is not the shore: Conversations toward a Buddhist-Christian awareness* (2001). In one essay, they engage the ideas of memory, Eucharist and death. And these three topics seemed particularly fruitful ground for rethinking the meanings and purpose of research in a spiritual context. So here, I would like to examine the idea that life and death are one continuous and eternal research and teaching moment, ripe with the possibilities of awareness of the essential knowledge of what Stepanik (2001) calls our "heartsongs," those things we desire to bring into being. And fundamentally, our perceptions about life and death hold important implications for our ability to engage teaching and research as spiritual endeavors.

Thich Nhat Hanh and Daniel Berrigan (2001) say this about the connections between life and death:

Life is a phenomenon, death is a phenomenon, and both together are life. And that is why when one has seen the real nature of things, he will acquire a kind of fearlessness—an attitude of calm—because he knows his death will bring no end to life . . . So the existence of reality transcends both what we call life and death . . . what we usually call death is only part of life. (p. 6)

What a particularly powerful insight for teachers and researchers, as we find ourselves working within classrooms and community contexts where we are continually faced with helping children and ourselves deal with life threatening health conditions such as attention deficit disorder and HIV/AIDS; where homelessness is all too often the daily reality for entire segments of our people; and where violence and war have taken on an increasing normalized way of being in our society. Such conditions are rapidly bringing the difficult realities of human life and death even nearer to us—and rendering us unable to turn our backs on the suffering it brings in its wake.

What would it take to invite an awareness of life and ultimately death—our own and others—into teaching and research practice in more insightful and explicit ways? It seems that in the Western world, we consider death in our lives as some type of enemy to be overcome and certainly something to be avoided for as long as possible! What we call the "good life" has no room for consideration of this thing called death. Interestingly, when we begin to unpack our collective desire to live good lives, we find very contested cultural spaces, with our contest and struggle being fundamentally about what a "good life" might even *be*, especially as we realize that the capitalistic race we've been running for bigger and better material goods, larger stashes of cash, and our near overwhelming pursuit of the American dream have not created the happiness we assumed would be its ultimate reward. Rihbany (1922) shows us the futility of our pursuits:

You call your thousand material devices "labor saving machinery," yet you are forever "busy." With the multiplying of your machinery you grow increasingly fatigued, anxious, nervous, dissatisfied. Whatever you have, you want more; and wherever you are you want to go somewhere else . . . your devices are neither time-saving nor soul-saving machinery. They are so many sharp spurs which urges you on to invent more machinery and to do more business. (as cited in King, 1967, p. 201)

The trends in research topics have followed a similar trajectory. As we look at the current hot topics in educational research and teacher education in this new millennium, the focus is largely on issues such as the devastating effect of violence in society, racial and ethnic difference, urban and inner-city schools and communities, poverty, and our newest nemesis, terrorism. Researchers "research," hoping to find appropriate responses to these social ills. Teachers research and teach as well, desperately seeking knowledge to respond to the ways in which these "ills" show up daily in the lives of the children they teach. But what is often prevalent in our research—and what we are all too often fascinated with—are the shadow side of the lives and contexts of those under study. In other words, we are fascinated not with the strength and *life* of these communities, but with the circumstances—deliberate or otherwise—that are inviting their demise, their death. Too seldom do we honor, through our study, the endless and incredible and resilient possibilities of life and work of people within these communities, brave men, women, and children who have not only reframed or even conquered their fear of death, but can bear witness to such transformation through great acts of faith, courage, and spirit.

But here is an often unanswered question for researchers. If we start from the premise that as human beings, life and death are not extraordinary events but instead part of the same continuum (and, thus, both deserving to be explored), what kinds of spaces might be opened for more expansive research foci as well as insight and awareness in our own lives and deaths as researchers?

I started this essay in December 2001, after returning to the United States from a pre-Christmas trip to Ghana. It was a particularly special trip, one that included the enchanted recognition of the man who would become the beloved in my life, my Henry. Having been born and raised in Ghana, he'd never been separated from the rich African cultural knowledge and traditions (as African Americans were through the horror of the slave trade). I continue to marvel at his ability to embrace the journey of life and its ultimate passage in death with seemingly little fear and with the grace of a man who deeply understands the historical and continuous nature of life and death as they manifest as near daily realities in Ghana, given the hardships of life in a developing country. "You see, life and death are the same thing, Cynthia," he said during one of the many long-distance calls across the sea that typified our courtship. "Your Dad is preparing to go and it's okay."

Henry was referring to the decline of my Dad's health—and the responses, reactions, and changing roles I was preparing to undertake as our family dealt with the multiple and complex meanings of my Dad's condition, through the toll that congenital heart failure and diabetes were taking on his body, mind, and spirit. Because I live in the state of Ohio and the rest of the family live in or nearer to Seattle, my involvement in the everyday caretaking for Dad was limited to occasional visits. Most often, it took the form of regularly talking to him on the phone, sharing jokes that cheered him, or updating him on the goings on in my life. And we always talked a lot more when it was the season for planting or tending the garden, something my Dad and I had enjoyed together as I was growing up. My other caretaking role was with my Mom who was engaged in the often daunting task of being the sole caretaker for Dad. With her, I listened to her frustrated descriptions of the headaches and the heartaches she felt, and the complex decisions she was making on a daily basis in light of Dad's needs. My younger sister Celeste, a registered nurse, was truly a blessing in our family. She was able to decipher the "medicaleeze" involved in Dad's near constant care, and was thus able to assist Mom in the day-to-day caretaking that my Dad needed, both inside and outside of endless hospitals. But returning from Ghana this trip—and recognizing that Dad's condition was becoming critical—brought long deliberations and discussions with him and with various health professionals about the need for a level of care that we could no longer provide at home. Just a week before Christmas, we moved him into a private nursing home—and made the commitment, as a family, to be there with him daily, to help create a new home for him in that space. So instead of the usual Christmas gathering in the family home, we spent Christmas in the party room of Kelsey Creek Care Facility. And by far, the hardest part for each of us was coping with the glaring fact that, while he remained cheerful in the face of increasing seizures and pain, Dad was rather quickly making his transition from the physical to the spiritual world.

A few days after Christmas, I visited my Dad for what would be the last time in this life. He lay there in the hospital bed, as if dreaming, a slight smile on his thinning face. We exchanged pleasantries as I fastened a new much needed elastic strap to his heavy eye glasses, adjusting them and laying his head on the hospital pillow. It had been a long time since I'd had such intimate moments with my Dad, one of the blessings of being with him during his final days. He asked about the progress of my writing, his modern-day version of the question he always asked when I was a child: "What did you do in school today?" We talked about Ghana, a place that was magical for him, but that he'd never had the chance to visit, due to the fragility of his health. And, he talked about how Christmas "wasn't the same in here." The depth of his statement seemed to refer not only to being in the care facility, but to the feeling of a change in his spirit, in his increasingly deteriorating body that characterized this moment in his life. During one of the many silences—something he and I had so comfortably shared for nearly 45 years—I realized that, as a family, what we really wanted was for him to stay with us, to never leave us. But he'd lived a full and happy life, "raised up" and provided a solid foundation for each of his now grown children, and left my Mom well taken care of. His work on earth was finished. Spiritually, it was time for him to return to the Creator. And in the silence of that moment, I was given the courage to release him. To let him go, knowing that the physical body was no longer useful for his work. "Daddy, I know you are tired of the trials and tribulations of this body," I said. "And when you are ready to go, you just go. We will all be fine." And my Dad looked at me, rather nonchalantly and spoke: "Oh, Cynthia. I know. I'm just so tired. When I'm ready to go, I'll make that decision. And there's nothing that anyone can do to change my mind." I marveled at his clarity: His spirit seemed truly at peace. I kissed his cheek and told him I loved him. Smiling brightly, he said in the dry manner that characterized my Dad's personality: "I know. You take care now." The lump in my throat finally gave way to a stream of tears as I walked out of the building. And five days later, my Dad died.

Having returned to our respective homes, we were all summoned back to Seattle. And as "the one who likes to write" and who "gives speeches," my Mom asked me to prepare and deliver the eulogy at my Dad's memorial service. It was not an easy task, but I revered in the opportunity to proudly speak of my father's life and work as a teacher, one that exemplified the strength and courage of a Black man born and raised in the segregated south in the 1930s. Interestingly, there was something very comforting about my father's death, the ultimate surrender of the body whose sickness and pain had plagued him for far too long. And given the growing interest and importance of spirituality in my life and work, I welcomed the opportunity to invite his always present wisdom and guidance into my life in a new way and to create a new relationship with him now on a spiritual versus physical plane. In death, what he'd given me was the chance to "re-member" his life, to put it together with my own in ways that so clearly provide the roadmap for how I have become who I am right now. Through preparing his eulogy, I was also able to enact an ancient ritual of mourning that gave me a place to put my grief and to honor his presence through naming the legacy he left behind.

Most children take for granted—and even expect—that we will experience the death of our parents. It seems an almost unspoken rule of the universe. But, just one week after my Dad's death, I received a call that not only broke that rule, but my heart as well: My 46-year-old elder sister, Octavia—the one who had sat next to me on the church pew just one week prior at Daddy's memorial service—was found dead in her apartment from obstructive lung disease, a serious condition that was not known to the family and maybe not even to her. But what I did know was that the very principle I had been exploring and writing about in this essay—life and death as one continuous and eternal moment of re-search—was made even more profound, more real. But what if the re-search, the searching again in heart spaces that were already pained by Dad's transition yielded me no "results," no explanations to help me stand and help my family to do so as well?

Again, I was called to prepare and deliver Octavia's eulogy. However, this time, the task seemed unnatural, almost unimaginable: She was my older sister, the one I followed, the one I looked up to. But both in the painful preparation of the eulogy and in the near year that it took me to find the courage to return to finish this chapter, I realized exactly what Hanh and Berrigan were saying: *That experiencing the death of loved ones calls us not to recognize death but instead to recognize life.* And when we choose to share the contributions and stories of the human journey of those who have died, we usher in a sacred space of relationship with them that recognizes both their life and death as part of the same event. Writing Octavia's eulogy provided a powerful example of how, when we embrace the intimately connected nature of life and death—when we re-search and consider deeply what we know with the added wisdom of experience—we can begin to see the divine order of life and death. And such seeing can spiritually transform our mourning of death to the powerful affirmation of life, one that is expansive, more fully human as well as divine.

Excerpts from the Eulogy for Octavia L. Dillard

"All praises to the Creator, one whom our family has learned over the past few weeks, has arms big enough to hold the depths of our sadness, arms that know the love and understanding of ages, arms that have gathered friends and family from all over the world to lend their support and love and humanity to us. Loosing those you love is the sort of sorrow that is poignant and personal, yet amazingly universal in nature. And we are grateful for your presence here to share in this celebration of Octavia's life.

I stood in this same space just two weeks ago, giving the family eulogy for our dad, Mom's husband, your relative and friend. And at that time, I said that we were somehow comforted by the natural cycle of things, a cycle that includes children outliving their parents. However, when Octavia died, the theory of a natural cycle of things no longer held. Today, it seems we are presented with two choices: We can curse God for going against the cycle of things. Or we can, even as we struggle, recognize and accept the fact that the cycle belongs to God . . . And whether you are 6 or 46 or 66, when it's time to join the Creator, it is time. And it was Octavia's time . . .

Octavia was an avid quilter. And one of the things that I re-member most about our elder sister is the careful way that she'd study and make very deliberate choices about the particular cloth in the quilts that she made. And in this celebration of her life, we are asked to make some choices of our own. We might choose to release from our hearts the bitterness, trauma, and sadness of what we see as Tave's death and understand her transition as part of the very thread of life, the true miracle that we are all living through. We might choose to accept that out of our grief and sorrow is coming deeper and deeper understanding, deeper and deeper love. We might choose to see that, in this hour of need, like Tave in life, God asks for no credentials before we can ask for help or strength. But in life and death, Octavia, like God, asks only for an invitation to continually be present at this party we call Life. She's already invited us hundreds of times—in our memories, in her beautiful photographs, in her art. Sending the RSVP back to her is up to us.

Finally, the last piece we might choose is maybe the hardest. We might choose Octavia's freedom and her newfound peace over our own pain. She is free now to do and be with God and all the ancestors and the angels—and with Dad. And, as Kahlil Gibran (1998) says in *The prophet*:

> . . . For what is it to die but to stand naked in the wind and melt into the sun? And what is it to cease breathing, but to free the breath from its restless tides, that it may rise and expand and seek God unencumbered? (p. 40)

The gift of life is to be graceful and artful in it. In the gift of her life, Octavia was both. There is no greater gift than giving our Octavia—and the art that was her life—back to the Greatest Artist of All. We love her and will miss her as we know that you will. But, more than that, we are grateful for the gift that her human journey was to the world . . ."

New Questions: A Matter of Life and Death

As a teacher and researcher, I often rely on my academic preparation and experience to make sense of the everyday happenings in my life. However, no amount of "rational" thought, intellectualizing, data analysis, or study could help me to understand why Dad and Octavia had to die when they did—or why they died so close together. But when they died, they helped *me* to understand that life is energy, changing places and forms all the time. And it matters not whether one is a researcher, the one researched, the one funding the research project. It is when people die that we so powerfully see that life as we experience it right now is happening on a spiritual level: The moment we are born, we begin to die. So the real nature of life is every day moving us toward death. And the openings that arise from letting go of the illusion of our *human* control of life and thus death, and surrendering to the best part of ourselves, which is God, allows us to understand an important truth: That every one of us is born at the perfect time and we each will die at the perfect time, to fulfill our appointed work on this earthly journey. And for those of us interested in teaching and research, what seems like punishment and unfair pain when suffering and death visit us are necessary and important opportunities for growth, for starting again, for re-search. The deaths of my beloved father and elder sister and their becoming my ancestors is not an abstract notion in my life and work: It is rather the catalyst for an intensely intimate emotional storm that is allowing me to access the inner wisdom needed to guide me through the vacuum their deaths have created.

In the two months that followed my Dad and Octavia's death, I took a medical leave and stayed with my Mom: I could hardly imagine what tragedy she felt inside, having lost both her husband of over four decades and her firstborn child. And during that time, when we could no longer find words to speak and had run out of tears to cry, we found solace in books about healing and death. In one of those books, *In lieu of flowers: A conversation for the living* (Cobb, 2000), the author recalls an interview that she did with Pulitzer prize–winning author Annie Dillard, as she herself struggled with how to write about the power of life and death. The advice Dillard gave her touched my soul: "Write as if you were dying," she said. "At the same time, write for an audience consisting solely of terminal patients. That is, after all, the case" (p. 84).

As teachers and researchers, ought we not be researching, teaching, and writing "as if we were dying?" Such a standard of rigor would require that we be ever vigilant in examining and tending to our body, mind, and spirit everyday—and that we be absolutely cognizant of our own short time on this planet. That we walk softly on the earth, including in the communities in which we do our work. That we embrace death, not as a sign of morbidity or pessimism, but as a portal through which we all will pass. That we conduct ourselves in such a way as to leave our students and others as though we may never meet again. Such practice would clearly help us to transform the ways that we act, talk, and interact with others. And it is a way for us to live in a conscious manner, recognizing that every moment that we have breath is an eternal moment, connected to all other moments past, present, and future. Thus, every moment can be a moment of re-search, of searching again, of change and growth in our spiritual lives. As bell hooks (2000) suggests:

> Accepting death with love means we embrace the reality of the unexpected, of experiences over which we have no control . . . We do not

need to have endless anxiety and worry about whether we will fulfill our goals or pans. Death is always there to remind us that our plans are transitory. By learning to love, we learn to accept change. Without change we cannot grow. Our will to grow in spirit and truth is how we stand before life and death, ready to choose life. (pp. 204–205)

And, at its essence, that is what research should be all about: About the lessons that come from the full circle of birth and life to death and life anew.

And what questions might these lessons ask of our academic lives? At the very least, we are asked to consider how we might choose to both stand within and engage in our work with a new set of questions, questions that focus less on our personal goals and more on the ways in which our work might foster our ability—and the ability of those we teach and work with—to stand before life and death, without an absolute desire for the former and an absolute fear of the latter. I am helped here in my thinking through Patricia Hill Collins's work (1998), where she articulated criteria for social theory and the work that we do as researchers where we might approach research in a way that really honors life, that seeks to do no harm and that helps us to face the tensions and the pain that are often a part of our work. However, in Colleen Capper's (2003) essay (that draws on Hill Collins's work), the spiritually nuanced way in which she asks the questions gives us a way to think about a new set of questions/criteria we might use as we consider life and death in our academic lives. Reflection and deep consideration of the following questions must become essential practice as we encourage teaching, research, and service that influences the spiritual lives of others as well as our own.

1. Does this experience of this life and death "mirror back to people the reality of their lives at a particular point in time?" (Capper, 2003, p. 197)

2. Does this experience of life and death "equip people to name their own pain and oppression for themselves, how they harm themselves, how they harm others, how they experience forgiveness of themselves and others, how they experience forgiveness themselves?" (p. 197)

3. Does this life and death "move people to question themselves and others, not to be critical but to seek to understand . . . also to experience joy, freedom and happiness?" (p. 198)

I would add a fourth question/criteria to Capper's list: *Does this experience of life and death provide a healing space within which love is generated and promoted?* Holding these questions/criteria for our academic lives, the final question may be the most difficult to face: If the answers are no to the questions above, what then is the use or purpose of an academic life?

5

Suddenly but Always Queen

Embracing a Methodology of Surrender in Research and Teaching

Situated in my own notion of an endarkened feminist epistemology discussed in Chapter 1, this essay steps outside the assumptions of social and identity theories that merely express one's "intellectual" pursuits and pragmatic concerns in research to theorizing research work in the world as having multiple and spiritual "points of affinity" (Appiah, 1992, p. viii). Arising from my ongoing research and subjectivity as an African American feminist scholar who was recently enstooled as Queen Mother in a village in Ghana, West Africa, I pose a fundamental question that should be of concern to researchers who recognize the deeply spiritual nature of our work, the ways in which considerations of the process of work (methodology) can open the way for profound relationships with spirit. The question, paraphrased from Rubin (1999) is this:

Who am I becoming as a researcher as I attempt to invent nothing (that is, to add no air or embellishments to my character or work) *or deny nothing* (that is, to embrace everything, making use of the strongest traits, energy, historical and cultural knowings in multiple and diverse contexts)? As we attend to this question, we both embrace the paradigms and principles that guide research of the spirit and consider consequent outcomes of our methodologies and practices. I explore here a *methodology of surrender* that seeks to embrace a research space that is both intimately meditative (that is, that listens and heeds the wisdom of the ancestors and the Creator) and faith filled (that is, prayerfully attentive and grateful to the spiritual world and the Creator.

"Call Me By My True Names (12)": Becoming a Queen Mother

And that's what learning is.
You suddenly understand [and remember]
Something you've understood all of your life
But in a new [and old] way." (D. Lessing in J. Cameron's *Transitions*, p. 128)

A sacred pilgrimage is commonly viewed in religious terms. One travels to a "Holyland" to celebrate and deepen one's personal and communal religious understanding and affiliation, a sort of grand tithing to a Higher Power. While I believe these journeys most often occur in religious settings, they too can occur in educational and secular settings. One such pilgrimage that is at once sacred, secular, and spiritual is the return of African-ascendant persons to the continent of Africa. I focus here primarily on such a pilgrimage, on a traditional African ritual ceremony of sacred inclusion: My enstoolment, as an African American professor, to Queen Mother of Mpeasem, a West African village in Ghana's coastal Central Region. This ceremony was and continues to be an important part of my ongoing work to re-search African ascendent knowledge and is offered in celebration of my deepening sacred relationship with such knowledge and an affirmation of an African ethos of spirituality.

In the ancient tradition of the various peoples of Ghana, a Queen Mother can literally be understood as a female king. She is chosen for this role by the elder head of the clan/family, the council of elders and other prominent people of the village community. For the Western mind, one might understand her role as "one who owns the state as a mother owns a child" (Jeffries, 1997). A Queen Mother is considered a divine being, a founder of the state who is able "to give life" and maintain life in her state. She rules along with the Chief of the Village and the Council of Elders. In ancient as well as modern times, Queen Mothers carry a staff with a wisdom knot in the center, a symbol of the wisdom that she quite literally "holds in her hands." Like the Chief and others who are a part of the paramount system, she is called "Nana" and receives, on the day of her enstoolment, the chosen name of a passed on ancestor and other symbolic gifts of gratitude and thanksgiving from the Chief and the village community, such as a beautifully carved wooden stool from which she reigns or a new piece of kente cloth. Given that I am one of the few diasporic

African ascendents who has entered such an ancient and revered institution, one thing was clear: When I "became" a Queen Mother, I wasn't making history; history was making me.

Becoming a Queen Mother (13)

You woke me this morning
And I became part of Your divine plan
Chosen on this day
To be among the living.
You dressed me in a purple kaba (14)
And I became the color of royalty,
Traveling to the village in a dirty old van
That felt like my royal carriage,
The curtains drawn for the privacy
Of the new Queen Mother.
You introduced "Professor Cynthia Dillard"
To the Chiefs of the kingdom,
And I became my own desire
To know as I am known,
You honored my family name
On the front of the community center and preschool,
And I became my parents, their parents, parents, parents,
Those who, by virtue of the Blackness of Africa
Were considered by some
Not to be fully human,
But whose depth of humanity shone like the sun in this moment.
You brought my sister-mothers to bathe me in the soothing waters of life,
And I once again became the child of all my mothers
Marion Lucille Cook Dillard
Wanda Amaker Williams
Florence Mary Miller
Nana Mansa, the first,
And those unknown to me.
You wrapped me in the swath of traditional kente,
And I became the weavers of that cloth,
The men who learned from their fathers
An art so special that it had taken months and months
Of skill, patience, and love in its creation.
You sat me on my Queen's stool
And I became Nana Mansa II, Nkosua Ohemaa (15)

The spirit of Nana Mansa I now residing not in my head,
But in the stool,
She speaks centuries of cultural memories
Directly to my heart, as an African American,
"I had many children, but you are the only one who has returned."
You lovingly dress me in beads old and new,
Adorning my fingers with gold rings, my Queen's chain around my neck,
And I became the precious riches and treasures of Your Universe
Now and then.
You fanned me with cloth and palms and bare hands,
And I became the wind
Carrying Your voice:
"Don't be afraid, Nana. Trust me. You have all that you need. I will
    show you what you already know."
You poured libation
And called me into the sacred ritual of remembering,
And I became my own full circle as a researcher,
A searcher again, honoring the knowledge of
Who and what is here and there
Of what's been and is to be,
Inseparable realities, united by Your gift of breath,
A committed teacher and student of my own becoming.
You drummed and we danced
And with each beat,
I became the rhythms of my passed on ancestors,
Who gathered with us on that day
Brothers and sisters of the village, the community, the diaspora,
A holy encounter indeed!
You gave food to feed the whole village,
And I became my own full belly,
And the too often empty bellies of the village children and families,
For that moment, we were all satisfied.
Full.
Happy.
Joyful in Your bounty.
You've blessed me with life,
A chance to manifest extraordinary works
Through You.
By becoming all of myself
I can live not into the smallness of the world's expectations
But into the greatness of the true names
You've given to me.

This meditation points to several important considerations relative to appropriate methodologies to engage research of the spirit, research that, from my point of view is necessarily a culturally based and qualitative activity. First, such qualitative research arises from deep, sometimes even intimate relationships between human beings and within human beings themselves. The researcher cannot actually engage in the research activity by studying or reading alone: He or she must experience the research, the searching again, in the company of others. Second, in qualitative work that attends to the spiritual and to research as service, it is often the case that we are visited by powerful desires in the course of our work, desires that we can't explain but that almost mysteriously move us to do something we never imagined. These might be seen as spiritual visitations. While Ghanaian culture (and interestingly, what we call "developing" cultures) often have philosophies and ways of dealing with such spiritual "visitations," too often in the name of objectivity or rigor, we researchers often name such arrivals as intrusions—and do all that we can to get rid of them! Unfortunately, in doing so, we often miss out on the gifts and insights that such desires, left to their work, would reveal to us. In this case, during the course of this research work, I didn't invent my becoming a queen mother, nor did I will it up from deep within my heart. In fact, there are certainly times when I didn't even want such a development to come and disrupt what I felt was a rather comfortable phase of my life and work. But, as a dear friend used to often say: "It's not easy to turn away a spirit on a mission"—and it's even harder to speak of the ways that such desires find their way into one's work! I am coming to realize in this re-search that becoming a queen mother required me to honor my desires and to receive this visitation of spirit, even as it required a major adjustment in my relationship to the village of Mpeasem, its people and, frankly to life itself, including my research. And in those adjustments were moments of profound insight, creative development, and shifts in the ways I fundamentally engage in research.

Thus, this endeavor called research is done not just in the abstract, but experientially, through spiritual practice creating praxis: As researchers, whether we choose to be in more intimate and human relationship with the subjects of our work and whether we choose to be subjects within the work ourselves will make the ultimate difference between the lessons we learn and the lessons we just "think about." And it will make a profound difference in how we conceptualize and engage methods that attend to the spiritual nature of our human relationships within our research.

Who Feels It Knows It All: Toward a Methodology of Surrender (16)

In many ways, this story is a very particular one: Of one African-ascendant woman researcher's journey and the ways that spiritual integrity—connections of mind, body, and spirit—have been "uncovered" within my life and work through my experiences in Ghana particularly and in the world generally. The thesis here is that these connections—"revelations"—would have been unavailable except through the real experiences of sitting still in meditation before and after my enstoolment or delightedly sharing a cold beer on the shores of Cape Coast or fiercely debating issues of identity and cultural politics between Africans living on the continent and African living in the diaspora. These experiences have certainly made me even more aware of who I am, whose I am, and of my life as a spirit-filled teacher, leader, and a researcher. However, even more important, they've provided ways to "read" more clearly and productively universal notions that arise from these particular direct experiences of communities of care and connection, across differences. And it seems to me that the more stories we "uncover," from multiple cultural spaces that we live within and through, the more able we might be to foster a balance of the spiritual, emotional, and intellectual development of ourselves and others in today's culturally diverse research settings.

Thus, we return to the central question of the paper: In examining my reality, who am I becoming as a researcher as I attempt to invent nothing (that is, to add no air or embellishments to my character or work) or deny nothing (that is, to embrace everything, making use of the strongest traits, energy, historical, and cultural knowings on both sides of the water)? And given those questions, what methodological practices will allow knowings to arise in ways that engage the body, mind, and spirit, bringing all to bear in service to communities in the world? Ultimately, these questions have required letting go of knowledge, beliefs, and practices that dishonor the spiritual research life presenting itself in/as/through me.

Such a path has lead me to explore a methodology of surrender, one that seeks to embrace an intimate research space that is both meditative (that is, that listens and heeds the wisdom of the ancestors and the Creator) and faith filled (that is, prayerfully attentive and grateful to the spirits and the Creator). Through this exploration, I have reconceptualized research as a process of shared readings between human beings that honors contemporary, historical, and spiritual knowledge of multiple continents and contexts of African presence. I suggest that one's perspectives are formed (morally, culturally, politically, spiritually) by the breadth and depth of the life one has known, focusing on those knowings that arise not only from European and New World conceptions of Africa and things African, but from reading the historical and contemporary manifestations of shared spiritual and indigenous cultural traditions and life as well.

Thus, in rethinking research methods, Freire and Macedo (2000) say this: "The starting point for a political-pedagogical project must be precisely at the level of the people's aspirations and dreams, their understanding of reality and their forms of action and struggle" (p. 214). Freire and Macedo go on to discuss a useful distinction between methods and our fondness for substituting "models" for them. A *method*, they suggest, is "a series of principles which must be constantly reformulated, in that different, constantly changing situations demand that the principles be interpreted in a different way" (pp. 216–217). In other words, the challenge to us as researchers—and to our work—is to translate the fundamental principles of our method *as the situation demands*, in ways that are ultimately and intimately more responsive and responsible to multiple and diverse situations. As I reflect on my own research purposes and practice, I see healing and transformation as the central goal of my research. Thus, generating and nurturing what at its essence is all about love (hooks, 2000) is the truly radical stance that such a healing and transformative purpose requires. Further, I have been deeply influenced by the work of Buddhist monk Thich Nhat Hanh, who helps me to see that unconditional love in the practice and methods of research is facilitated by our ability to let go or surrender the principles of objectivity, domination, patriarchy and inequity that have characterized the practice of research—including its methodologies. Thus, I put forth these four principles of a methodology of surrender that have been especially powerful in helping me to more productively read (Appiah, 1992) my own becoming as a researcher and the spiritual nature of re-search, given research work in both Ghana and the United States—and with attention to the spiritual world that is alive within that work. In the spirit of Freire and Macedo's voices above, these principles are not given as the prescriptive list for all research projects: They are shared as an example of engagement in spiritual re-search across differences, with particular emphasis on both the researcher and those participating in research developing and becoming more fully human in the process.

Love

Love is the intention and capacity to offer joy and happiness. According to Peck (1978), love is *"the will to extend oneself for the purpose of nurturing one's own or another's spiritual growth.* Explaining further, he continues: *Love is as love does. Love is an act of will—namely, both an intention and an action. Will also implies choice. We do not have to love. We choose to love"* (p. 4). hooks (2000) goes further, suggesting as I do that the missing element is the need to engage love as the *experience* that creates more reciprocal (and thus more just) sites of inquiry. This includes developing the practice as a researcher of looking and listening deeply, not just for the often self-gratifying rewards of the research project, but so that we know what to do and what not to do in order to *serve* others in the process of research. This also includes carefully seeking understanding of "the needs, aspiration, and suffering of the ones you love" (Hanh, p. 4). If we continue to offer to the communities we engage something that they don't need or readings and representations where they cannot recognize themselves or see themselves more clearly, we are not being as researchers in love with them or ourselves. Maybe more important, we have also not yet embraced the intimate nature of re-search that ultimately forces us to surrender our sense of separateness, to see ourselves in the lives of another.

Compassion

Compassion can be understood as the intention and capacity to relieve and transform suffering through our research work. This is not a principle that suggests that we must each suffer to remove suffering from others. Just as doctors or nurses can help to relieve a patient's suffering without experiencing the same disease, this principle suggests that researchers can also relieve communities of their suffering through the process of their work without being crushed by the weight of suffering and being rendered unable to help. Compassionate research contains deep concern for the community—and the desire to bring joy to those in the community through the work that we do. As researchers we must be aware of suffering, but retain our clarity, calmness, and strength so that we can, through our practice, help to transform the situation and ourselves.

Reciprocity

Reciprocity is the intention and capacity to see human beings as equal, shedding all discrimination and prejudice and removing the boundaries between ourselves and others. As long as we continue to see ourselves as the "researcher" and the other as the "researched" or as long as we continue to value our agendas for research as more important than the needs and desires of the community, we cannot be in loving, reciprocal relationships with them. Imagining one's self as another—and all of us as spirit beings having a human experience—is the only way to narrow the chasm between the "differences" that are so often the topics of our academic discussions and work.

Ritual

Ritual can be understood as the intention and capacity to transcend the boundaries of ordinary space and time or the practice of unifying the human and the divine. It is the process and desire to recognize, in the everyday work of research, the "eternal moment" (Richards, 1980) that is also present. As researchers, whether conscious or not, we are always one with reality, not removed from it, as has been the ethos of Western research traditions. And from an African worldview, when we engage in the practice of ritual in our work—in continuously and consistently re-membering the spirit of those physically deceased and now in the spiritual realm, those here in the physical realm, and those yet to be born—we honor the transcendental nature and experience of research that provides the renewal of energy and wisdom necessary to be researchers who engage our craft as the intellectual and spiritual work that it is.

Love, compassion, reciprocity, and ritual allow us to more clearly recognize humans in our various ways of being. But engaging these principles is not something that one can do easily or quickly: We have to *be* with the other, over time, with an open heart that is as eager and willing to engage in continuous re-search and self-transformation as we are in telling a particular research story. In this way, such principled relationships can be realized—and love, compassion, reciprocity, and ritual can be enacted in ways meaningful to the people and to the context.

But, as researchers, we all too often embrace the notion that we should remain the same in the project, just reporting or theorizing what we've seen. In becoming a Queen Mother, I learned that is not the case. Spiritually, researchers can also be transformed along the way. And if we are not spiritually transformed by the work that we do, we remain at the same point, engaging the same principles—the "way" that we began. However, in engaging a methodology of surrender as practice within a spiritually based paradigm, I've learned not only that the way of transformation (re-search) must be within you, but that the destination of the work—what you want the work to do in the world—must also be within you, not wrapped up in one's other agendas, space, or time. If such re-search/self-transformation is being engaged and realized, we *will* change and grow as human beings and certainly as researchers. What has helped tremendously in this work in Ghana is recognizing that human beings all over the world do many of the same things I do, *but in their own way.* Thus, I always learn from others and they from me. But more than that, like all research encounters, I am *spiritually* in need of their presence in my life: To share experiences, to support one another in difficult times (whether financial, spiritual, intellectual, etc.), to become, through the many encounters and engagements that we have. Our encounters with others are not random encounters: As spiritual beings (whose roles in life include that of teacher or researcher), we are having a human experience in relationship *with* others in our projects. But we are having our experiences in research because we *must* have them, because we've come to either be a teacher or student in each other's lives. Thus, our methodological choices are spiritual choices, interrelated and whole. Research and teaching become processes of give and take. But the challenge to our academic lives and work is to move beyond simply receiving (that is, getting something from others in the research encounter): It is also about what we can *give.*

6

Akwanbo

From Speaking Words to Inviting the Voice of Spirit in Research

*The power of the word is real whether or not you are conscious of it.
Your own words are the bricks and mortar of thr
dreams you want to realize.
Behind every word flows energy.*

—Sonia Choquette in J. Cameron's Heart Steps, p. 1

Research of the spirit is a way of life, a way of being in the world. It is a way of being that recognizes that, long before one is invited and introduced to the role and world of "researcher," one is invited and introduced to the world as a human being, a spiritual being engaged in an earthly experience. If we believe that each of us is endowed with a divine purpose for being and divine work that we were uniquely sent here to do, then any energy spent in reflection on the spiritual nature of our actions as researchers might be fruitful in transforming research into practice that also places the spiritual de-velopment of humanity as its central purpose.

But such reflection is not an easy task, especially for those of us who have embraced (consciously or not) the ideology inherent in our extensive research training. We are taught that the goal of research is to develop theories that can "explain" human phenomena. We learn to read the related work in the field, the research findings of other theorists. We survey the field of choice, selecting those pieces that ultimately justify the need for our own research studies. We then go to the field, rigorously looking, maybe participating, definitely documenting and gathering data from and about other human (spirit) beings, hoping to answer the research questions that are of interest to us. Finally, we "theorize," what we've seen and experienced, representing our best understanding of the deeper meaning of the lives of other human beings. After all is said and done, we have our research "findings," which can indeed be very useful to the field and even to advocacy work that leads to the "development" of the community (through changes in policy, new allocations of resources to the district, etc.). But, many of us also recognize just how inhumane the whole process can be for ourselves and for those who are the "subjects" of such a research encounter, as little attention is given to the essential spiritual existence and human nature of both the researcher and the "researched"—and the always partial nature of what we think we *know*. What happens to our research questions and consequent projects when we become aware that the "researched" are spiritual beings engaged in a human experience? And, what also happens to us as researchers when we recognize that we are as well? Freire .(1970) suggests that the fundamental purpose of all human beings is to become more fully human, to move toward our own freedom. This is a *spiritual* purpose. However, what our training teaches us is quite the contrary. We learn the "science" of research, becoming experts theoretically, methodologically, maybe even linguistically (that is, in the language of research). But we spend very little time speaking to, thinking about, and certainly sharing stories of what the research process *does to us*: How we *are* in the process of research and what we are learning about the condition of being human beings through our research relationships with other human beings. And what my continued presence in Ghana teaches me—and what I hear my soon-to-be-Ph.D. students in the United States telling me time and again—is that the heart desires a deeper connection to the work of research, to the very spirit of the endeavor: We need not only to know research and be in the world as researchers, but to also "open a way" for all of humanity to become more fully human as a result of our re-search endeavors.

Akwanbo: September 11, 2002

No more words. Hear only the voice within.

—Rumi, in J. Cameron's Heart Steps, p. 120

The gong-gong was sounded. The women and children of the village began to gather at the community center. Arriving a bit later were the men, having just completed a morning of communal labor in preparation for the upcoming funeral of the head of the village chief's family. My Nana stool was brought to the raised portion of the center, along with the skin-covered chair for Henry, who often serves as my translator (and is my husband—this is clearly work we've undertaken as a family!). The village elders sat on a wooden bench directly in front of us. As folk arrived, some came to greet me, kneeling and shaking my hand in a very reverent way: We exchange greetings in combinations of their limited English and my limited Fanti. "How are you?," "Me ho ye," "Nana, you are welcome."

Community meetings are the way information is commonly shared in Mpeasem. A community meeting can be called at any time by the Chief, Queen Mothers and/or Elders of the village. But this meeting was a bit unusual for me as it was the first community meeting that I'd called on my own and that was being held without the presence of the village chief.

Once gathered, it is custom for the person(s) who called the meeting to share the mission of the gathering. The chair of the school committee shared this mission as that of hearing from their queen mother, Nana Mansa II. At that time, he also designated himself as the interpreter. The scholar in me panicked a bit, knowing that his limited English ability might lead to some serious misinterpretations of the meanings of my words at best and absolute mistranslations at worse. But one of the things that being in Ghana teaches me is that in everything that I do, God and the ancestors are in charge. I straightened myself on the stool and began, thanking the Chair for his introduction.

My remarks on this day focused on the gift of life, given that the meeting was on September 11, 2002, the one year anniversary of the World Trade Center terrorist attacks that lead to the deaths of so many from all over the world. And while Ghana is a long way from New York City (and no libations were actually poured), I honored and raised the names of those who'd died in the attacks, as well as the names of my Dad and my elder sister, Octavia, who'd also died in January 2002. The ritual of honoring the dead and customarily sharing the news of my life since my last community meeting steadied me: I felt the power of the spirit within. I called on the community to understand the spiritual nature of life itself: As each of us had been granted by the Creator the gift of life on this day, we also had a responsibility to this community of Mpeasem. And service to this community was our "rent for living" (Edelman, 1992). One of my major responsibilities as Queen Mother is to help to develop and provide the best possible education for the children of Mpeasem, the ultimate future leaders of the village. But I reminded them, too, that this was not my work alone: It also belonged to them. That the privilege of having a preschool right in the center of the village brought with it the responsibility of not only sending their children to school, but also to paying their school fees as well. In this way, we needed to see development as a cooperative endeavor. Recounting our accomplishments so far, I reminded them of the many projects that had been requested and suggested by them—from planting flowers around the school building to electricity to an income-generating farming project. The work of development is for all of us to do, given our special talents and always on behalf of the children. "This is all I have to say," I said, a traditional way of conclusion. The crowd clapped with enthusiasm. But even in their applause, I knew that my words in English were not understood. Yes, I'd felt the connection that a common language provides with the one or two more of the more fluent English speakers. But deep down, I knew that my words were not comprehensible, a seeming waste of breath in my mind and heart. More than that, I felt sadness and frustration in knowing that even in a place where I hold an honored leadership role (and where people "know" me), my words were really a symbolic act: While they were literally heard, they were not literally understood. My message was lost on the very people I wanted to touch with my words.

But, as usual, tremendous insight came to me in this moment of inner turmoil, as it so often does when I slow down enough to listen: The Creator was showing me the incredible shortsightedness of my angst, the places where my ego and the false sense of power and importance I had placed on "words" (made concrete in my academic life), was not useful in this moment. Yes, it was *my* desire to have *my* words "understood" in a literal way. But God reminded me in that moment that words don't belong to me, and are always *created* for any given occasion and for a divine purpose. And, on this day, it wasn't the literal purpose that was the work, the purpose that we are most often rewarded for as academics. Instead, on that day, they served a *spiritual* purpose. These words, while not understood literally by most people of the Mpeasem community, were used this day to *set the tone,* to open the spiritual environment of the gathering. My reason for being there was not to "profess" or to even share the details of the various development projects, but to spiritually *gather* the people, in the sense that Paul D talked about his relationship with Thirty-Mile woman, in Toni Morrison's (1987) book, *Beloved:*

> She is a friend of mind. She gather me, man. The pieces I am, she gather them and give them back to me in all the right order. It's good, you know, when you got a woman who is a friend of your mind. (p. 272)

Said a different way, the words given to me that day didn't do the actual work of informing, but instead set the context for the work of informing *to be done by others more able to do it.* And, in a real sense as human beings, it's rarely the work of our words, but of the humble deeds that follow our words that often do the work of service within a community. Here, it was not the profundity of my words, but because of the resources (human and otherwise) that I have been gifted to bring together, that allows the work of development in Mpeasem to continue and sometimes even flourish. Resources like Henry, who, right after me, spoke for about 40 minutes, flushing out the details of "Nana's" talk, details that culturally as well as linguistically, my words in English could not carry but the spirit of his language and knowledge of my desires could. Resources like the teacher of the preschool, who could be given the "floor" to give a powerful speech that he might not have had the opportunity—or the courage—to do so under any other circumstances than with the permission of the Queen Mother. Resources like the assembly man, who was asked of the district level contribution to Mpeasem—and who had to finally make real commitments (of a public restroom) that had been long in coming. Resources like the elders, who lent the wisdom and experience of those who knew the importance of education to development and access to opportunity. One after another, these village leaders spoke—and the community added its voice—to the importance of education and the school in Mpeasem, and the responsibility of the community to continue to create it into a viable and vibrant site of activity and learning.

In our research and teaching projects, from a spiritually engaged perspective, I believe that we might begin to see the words that we use as an *invitation* for all involved to become more fully human through our research and teaching. According to *Webster's dictionary* (2001), to invite is: "1) to request the presence or participation of;

2) to request politely or formally; 3) to act as to bring on or to make probable; 4) to attract or entice." (p. 240). And when we think about invitation in a spiritual framework, there is an important human outcome of inviting another into the teaching and research endeavor. In the Akan language of Ghana, a phrase is often used in celebrations and festivals, especially those celebrating the human and material development work of the Nkosuaohene (Chief of Development) or Nkosuaohemaa (Queen Mother of Development). The phrase is *akwanbo,* which translates into English as "clearing the way." Our words, divinely inspired and heartfelt, can indeed clear a way to a different kind of relationship with one another, a different way of being in community: This is how spirit works. The Creator uses us, works us, does work through us that opens the way for us to do our work in the world. And as researchers and teachers, I agree with Asante (1988) that words are epistemic: That the words themselves are the physical manifestation of the divine ideas we hold in our head and heart. That means that the very words that we use have power and do their work *spiritually,* whether we are giving a conference presentation, having a conversation with a colleague, teaching our students, or engaged in the everyday work of living. Our words have the power to open the way for our humanity and the humanity of others to, as I heard Maxine Greene suggest, to "pull up a chair and sit down."

But what it also means is that the very purpose of research—from its conceptualization, to its methodology, from it's processes to its representation—must go far beyond words and the often meager and selfish purposes of personal careers that we often attach to it: Undertaken with the spiritual intent of opening a way to be of service to people and the life of the community, research takes on a larger, even transformational role, one that moves us beyond the "old tried and true spinning of scholarly wheels" (Hull, 2001, p. 252). *Our words can create what we want in the world.* And as one grows spiritually more focused as a re-searcher, our words gain even more power to affect those around us, to actually serve, transform and ultimately to heal.

What if, as researchers, we spiritually approached our research projects—and our relationships with others in these projects—knowing and confident that our words instead of our credentials were divine invitations to be in relationship with another, invitations that were able to both heal and serve? How then might our words, as

researchers, "clear the way" for others to be in more equal and satis-
fying relationships with us, relationships that focus on service, on
spiritual development? How might we more consciously and explicitly
acknowledge the power of spirituality in our intellectual activity, in
places that find it so difficult to consider and to trust "the substance
of things hoped for, the evidence of things unseen?" There are no easy
answers to these questions, only much reflection and maybe even
transformation for each one of us to do. And as the title of this
chapter suggests (and to both paraphrase and borrow from two of my
favorite books, the Bible and a novel entitled *Sarah's Psalm* by Florence
Ladd (1996): "I will [continue to] lift my eyes [across the seas] from
whence cometh my help. My help cometh from Ghana [and the
Creator] which is heaven and earth" (p. 292). As an African ascendant—and in these critical times—humanity deserves more than just
words from us.

7

Out of My Darkness I Find My Light
Naming Self, Naming Spirit

I can remember the day as if it were yesterday. I'd put on my favorite lime green and purple pants outfit and matching head wrap, hoping the clothes would help me not feel so damned conspicuous in the market. My friend Ma Vic gathered her plastic baskets and covering cloths, and along with the other village mothers, we piled into the van. Michael, the driver, teased every mother in the van, including me: It was part of the weekly ritual that I'd come to know as going to the market. Ma Vic, with whom I stayed during my time in the village, was not only my dear friend, but my guide in the maze of the market. She had her favorite sellers: The woman from whom she bought baskets of plump red tomatoes, another woman her plantains, another her yams, still another her spices and food staples. And as a regular customer, her loyalty was rewarded with the expected "dash" of a few extra onions or an additional handful of rice. As Vic confidently maneuvered her way through the market, I warily negotiated the open sewers, the sharp corners of the metal roofs, and the young market women who, without a stall, carried big trays of fish or mango or other goods on their heads. So, my eyes faced downward most of the time, tenuously watching every step. My observations of the market were primarily at the places where we stopped to make a purchase, the places where my eyes could focus on what was around me and not on my feet.

We stopped at the plantain woman's stall. "My sister!" the woman exclaimed, greeting Vic with the enthusiasm of someone who knows she's going to make a big sale. "You are welcome," she said to me, the customary greeting in Ghana when you haven't seen someone for a while. Her smile was warm, seeming to remember my presence on previous visits to her stall. Exchanging more small talk in Twi, Vic and the woman began their search for the biggest and the best plantains in the pile. And that's when our eyes met. About 70 years old, this woman (possibly the aunt or mother of the seller) was sitting in the shadows of the stall. She stared at me, a clear combination of curiosity and suspicion in her eyes, yellowed with age. She looked me up and down. I smiled at her, uncomfortable with her unwavering gaze. As Vic and the seller were finishing their transaction, the old woman reached over and touched Vic's arm, her face now absolutely perplexed, nodding in my direction: "What *is* she? Is she a white woman?" I nearly fell over, a rush of emotions running through me, from absolute horror to disgust to disbelief to sadness. Vic giggled and explained to the woman (who had still not quit staring at me) that I was not a white woman but a Black American (17). But that evening in my researcher's journal (and through confused, angry, and sad tears that could've filled a river), I wondered aloud as I wrote: "How could she see *me* as a white woman?" "Couldn't she see the African woman I could see in myself?" "Didn't she know what had happened to millions of Africans who'd been forcibly taken from the shores of Ghana and other West African countries?" "Where did she think we had gone?" "Had she never imagined that some of us would return?" "How can this sister/mother see me this way?" In reflection, what frightened me most about her question was that, at that very moment, I couldn't answer it myself:

> What had been the rather solid taken-for-granted nature of my African American identity—an identity that I'd used to make sense of myself—melted down like butter on a hot summer's day in that moment in Ghana. Something very rich that I loved dearly had become useless fat on the sidewalk, no help whatsoever in explaining and understanding what she saw, or who I was. But I know there is wisdom in her question or it wouldn't have come to teach me a lesson. If I'm to "be" a researcher in this space, I will have to struggle with the butter on the sidewalk, the shifting ground of African identity through Ghanaian eyes. Neither here nor there (Ghana or the United States), neither African nor American, neither recognizably Black nor white. Maybe it's not either/or: Maybe it's both/and? Somehow, it feels like it's be-

yond these dualities. They seem too simple. Regardless, it hurts to do this work. (Journal, 1/22/98)

And this pain stayed with me until the following week, when market day came again:

> Today is market day again. Honestly, I'm dreading it. But I don't think there's an acceptable excuse not to go and help . . . As we approached the plantain seller's stall, my stomach churned and my nerves were shattered, afraid of what "insult" (however innocent) would come from the old lady. Vic, oblivious to my inner turmoil, greeted the plantain woman and went about her business. But before I could properly greet the seller, I glanced to my right and caught the eye—and the smile— of the old lady. "Morning Black American lady! How are you?" she says happily, clearly concentrating hard to speak to me in her heavily ac- cented English. I replied "Me ho ye," Twi for "I'm fine." And she reached over and grabbed my wrist. "Black American. Yea." (Journal, 1/29/98)

As African American women scholars, most of us have lived our lives in a world where, as Du Bois (1989) suggests "there is ever an unasked question; unasked by some through feelings of delicacy; by others through the difficulty of rightly framing it. All nevertheless flutter round it, the real question . . . How does it feel to be a prob- lem? I answer seldom a word" (pp. 1–2). This question accurately describes the deeply raced, often bitter negotiations in the landscape of African American women's academic lives, historically and con- temporarily. The plateau described by Du Bois above is familiar ter- ritory for me, whether in Ghana or in other contexts. It echoes his notion of the sense of double consciousness,

> the sense of always looking at one's self through the eyes of others, of measuring one's soul by the tape of a world that looks on in amused contempt and pity. One ever feels [her] twoness—an American, a Negro; two souls, two thoughts, two unreconciled strivings; two warring ideals in one dark body, whose dogged strength alone keeps it from being torn asunder. (p. 3)

Again against the backdrop of white supremacy and the historical oppression of African ascendent people (particularly in the United States context), many African American scholars and writers have

articulated the power of Du Bois's metaphor of double consciousness
in accurately describing Black and white constructions of racial identity and the African American experience (Woodson, 1990; Ellison,
1952; Wright, 1945; Hurston, 1978). However, as we turn our eyes
and work toward Ghana and other African contexts and Du Bois's
(1989) idea of reconciling and "merging one's double self into a better
and truer self" (p. 3), I was still left with my own unanswered question, echoed in the story of the elder Ghanaian woman and my response to her characterization of my racial/ethnic identity and my
overwhelming response to it: "*Somehow, it feels like it's beyond these
dualities. They seem too simple. Regardless, it hurts to do this work.*" So
I would like to explore here the complexities and possibilities of
African American identity and Du Bois's notion of double consciousness when located not in the white racial landscape of the
United States but the African racial landscape in Ghana. Through
this exploration, I seek to share what I believe are some limitations
of Du Bois's notion of double consciousness in capturing the complexity and again, the possibilities, of an identity beyond nation
state, ethnicities, or other racialized constructions of difference.
Further, I will raise his often ignored notions of the spiritual and
physical underpinnings of race and the dialectic they create in our
contemporary meanings of racial and even feminist identities. Finally, I'll argue that beyond both biological and cultural explanations of identity, recognition of the spiritual nature of identity begins
to address our overreliance on race as an identity—and toward
possibilities of moving through and maybe beyond race to a more
equitable and subjective identity as human beings.

Beyond Double Consciousness

Consciousness, according to Greene (1988) involves "the capacity to
pose questions to the world, to reflect on what is presented in
experience . . . Human consciousness moreover, is always situated; and
the situated person, inevitably engaged with others, reaches out and
grasps the phenomena surrounding him/her from a particular vantage
point and against a particular background consciousness" (p. 21).

Greene (1988) goes on to say that consciousness is always partial, always changing, as human beings gather bits and pieces of new

information and new realities. Most important, she suggests that within the notion of consciousness lies a strong sense of vision, the ability "to look at things as if they could be otherwise" (p. 3).

From Du Bois's (1989) perspective, for African Americans, the world has historically denied such self-consciousness to develop: We have existed in "a world which yields [the African American] no true self consciousness but only lets [her] see [her]self through the revelation of the other world" (p. 3). As we look at the narrative of my encounter with the elder lady and my own identity, neither Greene's notion of self-consciousness nor Du Bois's double consciousness seem sufficient in explaining either the Ghanaian woman's question of my identity and personhood nor the emotional, intellectual and cultural meltdown of my own identity as a result of her question. It is clear that even with years of careful research, study, and lived experience as a Black feminist and multicultural scholar in the United States, I had constructed an identity that indeed embodied Du Bois's double consciousness (in trying to "fit in" to the Ghanaian context), in the shifting spaces where, as he suggests, I continued to seek "that tie that I can feel better than I can explain," in search of a place called home. Yes, I had indeed come face-to-face with "another world." However, at least part of my angst lay in having come face-to-face not with another world which was white (as I had all my life in the United States): For the first time in my life, another world was *Black*. Intellectually, culturally, spiritually, I had come face-to-face with Ghanaian consciousness and culture, an African space of understanding, identity, and knowledge that did not emerge from a space of striving or limitation or yearning for something: African consciousness comes from a place that is whole, has deep roots, and a richness of meaning and abundance historically and contemporarily. In other words, my self-defined identity as an African American now rested (and wrestled) in a context where I was not defined (at least in the same way) by others as a "problem" or personally, as Du Bois's suggested earlier, as one who was always "measuring one's soul by the tape of the world that looks on in amused contempt and pity." Instead, the meanings of my African American woman identity had come to meet Ghanaian consciousness, requiring a deeper knowing of the African in my own construction of my ever shifting identity locations. And it was the realization of how little both the old Ghanaian lady and I knew of the diversity of African identity on both sides of the water that was the furtile ground for pursuit of that knowledge.

When Two Souls Meet: Making Sense of Identity

Who is she?

> I bought some gorgeous purple cloth with gold embossed designs yesterday. So we rode the taxi to the tailor's place in Community 4 (not that that matters as I still don't know one community from the other!) after church this morning. Vic, Kwabi (her four-year-old son), and I walked several blocks, around corners and through alleys and little roads, passed groups of leering young brothers whose eyes followed our church-dressed hips all the way down the block! We finally got to the seamstress's place and were ushered into her room. Vic did introductions so quickly that I didn't catch the sister's name, but she was eight to nine-months pregnant. We selected a kaba style, a style Ma Vic said "suits me." We finished our business with Vic admonishing the seamstress not to "disappoint her" (by not having the dress ready on the appointed date, by spoiling the cloth, etc.).
>
> We'd gotten about a block away when I realized that I hadn't ordered head gear. While I waited with Kwabi, Vic ran back to do so. When she returned, she was giggling. "You know what? She was talking about you. She said [to some other folks who lived in the compound] that Americans always want the Ghana things here. And she says it's funny because they [African Americas] always want to come here and we [Ghanaians] are all trying to get to America! . . ."
>
> Later that evening, Vic and I talked about how people immediately know I'm American. "I think its your structure (the word used in Ghana to describe your height, weight, etc.)," she says. "And then it may be your color—but we have fair people too in Ghana here!" She continues to ponder: "Maybe it's your [natural] hair?" Then I jumped in: It's in my walk, the way I carry myself, and of course in my language and accent as soon as I open my mouth! I really noticed it today: In my clap rhythms in church (on two and four, like most Black folk in the states); in my height, as I tower above most Ghanaian men and women; in the very way my body's put together. It is as European as it is African in many ways, sturdy

and long, the embodiment of a certain kind of grace and elegance . . . Again it's that idea of hybridity—of knowing what you are the way you *are* it, given those historical circumstances from which there is no escape, which define the very essence of you. An amalgamation. Some of this, some of that. Sometimes the best and the worst of both and all parts. This too is about thinking again the notion of a Black American: It's meanings here in Ghana, its meanings in the United States, its meanings as I traverse both "homes," trying to do so with relative ease given the gifts of both places.

(Journal 1/18/98).

Who she is

It's been lights off (no electricity) since about seven P.M. Around seven-thirty P.M., the seamstress arrives with my dresses. They are both really beautiful. But so was what happened with the purple kaba: That was truly amazing! The seamstress asked me to go and try it on so she could make any adjustments that might be needed. Given my experience with the old lady in the market and the conversation Vic had overheard about African Americans wanting things Ghanaian, I was a little leery about what she might say once I put the dress on. I carefully tied my head wrap and tentatively came out of the side room. "Mmmmmm," she exclaimed, looking at me in my kaba, clearly in admiration. "Who tied it for you?" she said, pointing to my head wrap. "I did it," I said, realizing that I had done so in a manner that surprised her. "Turn around," she said sternly. And as her hand brushed down the back side of my body, I knew that, like the brothers earlier in the day, she too recognized one of the many carryovers of African womanhood that could not be oppressed or suppressed, even through the violence of the slave trade: The African woman's ass. She turned to Vic: "She *is* an African woman." So, however weak our identifications of these links between us, as African women, they were clear and apparent to her and me in that moment. And her look of recognition is one I will never, ever forget.

(Journal, 1/22/98)

Freire (1970) is right: Humanization is our primary vocation. Life is about seeing ourselves as human beings, in all our subjectivity, and involving one another in working toward the "better, truer self" that Du Bois (1989) suggests is an ongoing spiritual striving, particularly for African Americans. However, I would like to suggest here an important lesson embedded in the narratives in this chapter and throughout this book: Dualities, especially related to identity are wholly insufficient in explicating the complex, dynamic hybrid nature of African (American) identity. Even the more inclusive both/and identity position that I have traditionally marshaled from Black feminist thought cannot fully address the persistent nature of the dynamism that is inherent in our claims of identity. While I recognize the often dialectical nature of the meanings of relationship that mark human situations, being in Ghana has troubled the meanings further, by placing them within/against an African cultural milieu that I have claimed for at least part of my academic life, that is within/against an African (American) identity. In many ways, my relationship with Ghana has made it impossible to live within the dichotomies of identities that even I have taken for granted. For example, placed within/against the Ghanaian identity context, what becomes the meaning of Black and white, rich and poor, third world and first world, educated and uneducated when an African of the diaspora metaphorically places these gifts at the feet of Mother Ghana? In Ghana, I'm not African American, but Black American—but sometimes I'm even a white woman! In terms of a personal identity, neither the both/and (of my constructed critical feminist identity) nor either/or (of my African American identity set against the United States racial context) helps to make much meaning. And in the United States under no circumstances would I be categorized as a white woman! What becomes clear then is that identity is always about reading a situation, possibly even engaging in a shared reading (Appiah, 1992), where interpretations are mediated. And it is in these interpretations that possibilities for creating meaningful identities exist.

In the first narrative of the exchange between the elder Ghanaian lady and me, she read my identity as a white woman, in a way that was in total opposition to my own reading of myself as an African American or Black woman. While the relation exists between two apparently opposite positions, one could presuppose *mediation* between them. The woman had come into contact with something/someone (me) through a direct experience: She'd become conscious of me. My self-proclaimed identity (African or Black) is clear to the woman only to the extent that she can recognize me and see some resemblance between me and others known in her own lived experience to be African (American) women (as in the story of the tailor). One might say that, given the African context, the reality of my African identity emerges from others' encounters with it, with me: *It becomes as it is experienced and named.* This is what I mean by a mediation: Something that happens in the space *between* Black and white, between African and American, between people "educated" in differing ways—but something *that needs the other to make sense of itself.*

I Am Because We Are: Naming Spiritual Identity as Resistance

After a sabbatical, faculty at our university are entitled to teach a doctoral seminar that focuses on the research that was undertaken on sabbatical. As I was writing this manuscript and continuing my work in Ghana, I taught a seminar during the spring quarter titled "The Cultural, Spiritual and Intellectual Foundations of Education in Ghana, West Africa." In true seminar form, I had eight students who represented a wide range of racial, social, cultural, and international identity locations. In this seminar, students read drafts of various chapters of this book, along with other relevant texts from throughout the diaspora and the continent of Africa. And it was from one of our many discussions of "the book" that I began to see the weight of cultural, feminist, and racial identities—and the limits of their usefulness in really rethinking the very purpose of an academic life, especially one that attempts to bridge not only critical social justice concerns but African and African American spirituality and identities as well.

We were reading a chapter on the African view of personhood (Paris, 1995) and a draft of Chapter 3 of this book (on the building of the preschool and the power of the work in shaping new perspectives on teacher education and its purposes). Danielle (one of the students in the class who was concurrently taking another doctoral course on critical/feminist theory, equity, and diversity with me), excitedly came to class that evening. I began the discussion with an observation that came to me as I'd reflected on my own writing and while reading the Paris chapter: That something about my thinking and thus my writing seemed to be in transformation even as I wrote it. Danielle's hand was the first in the air. "I think I know what it is!"

she said with her usual enthusiasm for her own emerging sense of
African-centered thought. "With this chapter, I noticed that you and
the village and the work are becoming one thing. All through the
meditation you refer to all of it as "*we* did this" and "*we* did that."
And it's not like you're trying to become a Ghanaian, but you're
working like Freire says "*with* the people" (emphasis added). I had not
noticed this transformation in my writing. "Wow!" I said. "I hadn't
even noticed that! The transition that I became aware of has actually
left me in a bit of a dilemma. What I noticed was that the more I
center my thinking and academic work in African and spiritual knowledge and experience, the further it seems to be taking me from Black
feminist thought. I seem to be able to find enough "room" in African-
centered thought (with its attention to balance, harmony, spirit, wholeness) not to dismiss feminist thought but to background it somewhat."
And while it may seem on first glance that these are very different
concerns about identity positions and African notions of personhood,
in reflection, the transformations are part of the same dilemmas that
our current notions of racial and gender identity fall into—and that a
spiritual notion of identity might begin to get us out of.

   If we see an identity, mentioned earlier in the chapter as "a
coalescence of mutually responsive (if sometimes conflicting) modes
of conduct, habits of thought, and patterns of evaluation" (Appiah,
1992, p. 174), we can recognize that it is constructed, even invented,
sometimes with an abundance of inaccuracies, perpetuated by both
the person claiming it and those attempting to read it. The problem
is that identity, as constructed by most of us (including Du Bois) still
rests primarily on biologically rooted ideas of race: That being biologically "African" whether on this continent or the continent of Africa
or beyond automatically creates an African unity or African identity.
While it may seem that I am arguing against my own attempts to find
within an academic life my own African soul, it is what Du Bois
suggests—that which "I can feel better than I can explain" that is
precisely the point: Being African (or African American, or German
or whatever) is, for those who make the claim, only one of many
salient identities and ways of being from which we choose at any
given time. We constantly argue for, reframe, and reshape our identities as we theorize their multiple meanings. In fact, that seems to be
the real work of plenty of our academic discussions of identity, that

is constantly revising the meaning of identity. However, what I am suggesting—and what I continue to realize as my academic life more deeply centers in Ghana—is that the real struggle for identity is not being waged in the academy: It is being undertaken in the ethnic, political, oppressive violence that shapes the world of power and that I saw in the eyes of the elder Ghanaian woman or in the comments of the the seamstress in this essay. As Appiah (1992) so poignantly asks: "I wonder how much good it does to correct the theories with which these evils are bound up [when] the solution is food, or mediation, or some other material, more practical step" (p. 179). He goes on to say that while the economic interests often wrapped up in our constructions and theorizing about how identity operate through ideologies, "We cannot change the world simply by evidence and reasoning, but we surely cannot change it without them either" (p. 179). He suggests that it is the cultural products of resistance that are shared across African (American) culture that may hold that potential.

My student Danielle's recognition of the spiritual nature and importance of solidarity, my own musings about the usefulness of identity and Appiah's sage wisdom about our overtheorizing of racial versus cultural spaces for African people bring me to this realization: As scholars, we might turn our attention away from the notion of identity (that is, from the idea of becoming experts or scholars of identity), to being more deeply engaged in the spiritual nature of identity. These are two very different things. Any professors or teachers or scholar of identity who has managed to can keep their academic life uninterrupted and untroubled during the last few years of life in a world filled with the epidemic of HIV/AIDS destroying life on the African continent, unaffected by the continued devastation of our worldwide ecosystems, ignorant and unaffected by the wars raging in Afghanistan and Iraq (and plans for continuing this trend among world leaders), untouched by continued high rates of unemployment and underemployment (not to mention the continued use of child labor throughout the world), and unphased by terrorism and fear as a way of structuring life for all, can only bring trouble to their students, with a focus on intellectualizing and becoming "expert" on identity while the lives of so many are precariously hanging in the wind.

Let's consider, for a moment, a very different milieu in our discussions of identity. I believe it is possible—and being in Ghana shows me—that standing a different milieu provides another way of being, of becoming. For many, this discussion will feel as if it is a move against research, against scholarship, against an academic life. However for me, an academic life is a life that embraces and examines not just the words and the concepts but what is *within* the words, the ways that the words help us to be with others in mutually beneficial and loving ways.

Buddhists speak of karma as a fruit or as a seed. The seed of karma is one's action or being and the fruit of karma is what comes as a result. And when we hold up our heroes and sheroes, what we very quickly recognize is that we know them partially by the greatness of their deeds. However, it is not just their great deeds. We also recognize great leaders by what they have said. Maybe more important, we know them by *how* they have said it. We *feel* their identity, that coming together of words and deeds as the congruence between their talk and their walk. But if we try to analyze and find out the deeper meanings of their words without understanding the nature of the relationship between the one who has spoken and the one who is listening, we miss out on the deeper knowledge that the person has offered—and his or her humanity as well.

Paris (1995) states that African understandings of social and cultural identities carry with them the weight of lived situations, the weight of memory, and the weight of history. And such understandings also carry with them the weight of judgment as well. Understanding identity at the level of spirit requires moving beyond theorizing it: It requires compassionate engagement, a kind of engagement that requires one to continue to stay with the "melted butter on the sidewalk," the angst of not knowing who you are as an intellectual and seeing that as an opening to knowing who you are spiritually. I end this chapter with a wise but short story by Thich Nhat Hanh (Hanh & Berrigan, 1975):

> We are taught to look at a tree or something like that for a long time. At first you don't know what use it is to look at a tree like that. You have to look until you can truly see it. And one day the tree reveals itself to you as a very substantial, real identity. It is not that you have a new tree or that the weather is better so that you can see the tree clearly, but something in oneself has changed so there is a new kind of relationship between you and the tree. Whether we can see the tree or not depends on us. (p. 137)

He goes on to say that the relationship between human beings is or can be like that too:

> It's not because you have some education that you can recognize a human being in his [or her] various aspects. You have to be with him [her] a lot, with a kind of open attitude, a kind of continuous self-transformation in you before such a relationship is possible, is fully realized. (p. 137–138)

That is an identity that we might *all* be able to live with.

8

Coming Full Circle

Creating and Being on Purpose

> For four hundred years African creativity has been struggling to counter the narrow constraints of oppression, to circle it, turn it around, to seek order and meaning in the midst of chaos. My soul looks back in wonder at how African creativity has sustained us and how it still flows—seeking, searching for new ways to connect the ancient with the new, the young with the old, the unborn with the ancestors.
>
> —Tom Feelings

The phrase "coming full circle" is a very sacred phrase and is a way to express the uncovering of the very purposes and possibilities of my life generally and an academic life more specifically, having traversed the places and spaces of research, teaching, and service work in Ghana, West Africa, that have been discussed throughout this book. And in this final chapter, I want to explore, in a very intimate way, the meanings of these uncoverings in shaping an academic life and career. What is clear and important is to try to articulate this rather intimate understanding of full circle "as primarily a practice ordered by spirit, or authorized by spirit and executed by someone who recognizes that she cannot, by herself, make happen what she has been invited towards" (Some, 1997, p. viii). This includes a recognition that, as people of African ascent throughout the diaspora, we can only really live into our greatness when we *re-member* (that is, put back together) and respect the spirit within, our own brilliance, as human beings, and the grace inherent in the Creator's gift of breath.

The idea of coming full circle came to me one day in Ghana, West Africa, as I was walking through the Elmina slave dungeon with my Mom and my Aunt. In the reception area of the dungeons, there was an oil painting in very bright colors depicting a brutal scene of Africans captured and in shackles on the "final" journey through the "door of no return" (18). And a thought came into my mind that would change my life forever, and it is this: *When any person of African ascent chooses to return to the knowledge and motherland of Africa, we have in that brave act, come "full circle."* How powerful it was on that day to recognize that even those little doors of no return could not keep African people away from the place of our original breath!

"What between Africa and America and my soul constitutes at tie that I can feel better than I can explain?" asked Du Bois (1986) at the beginning of this book. And coming full circle has become a mantra, a metaphor, and a response to this question. And it is a description of the transformation that has so slowly and gracefully occurred in my academic life—and in the academic lives of many intellectuals of African ascent as we begin to make conscious and committed connections to Africa. The soul work that happens in experiences like that above in the slave dungeons—and illustrated throughout the pages of this book—help me to see the way that every experience in our lives is sacred and the coming together of all of life's experiences is but preparation for what ever happens next in our lives. That is full circle work.

My first trip to Ghana was with a group of educators. One of the benefits of going on an organized tour that focused on schools and educational settings was that I could see and extend my own experiences of the meanings and environments for learning, as they manifest in sites all over the country. And, as an educator, I was comfortable interacting and being primarily in primary schools and universities: While recognizably located in the cultural milieu of Ghana, they were somehow familiar, similar, and known to me. And like many schools that I've visited all over the world, these sites mirrored my work in the United States as a faculty member in multicultural teacher education, preparing teachers for diverse populations of students in elementary schools. But it was when I stepped outside of teaching courses at the University of Cape Coast or being with children in primary schools in Ghana and began to really see the country, to really talk and interact with people of various communities, that I began to open to spirit, began to recognize the powerful role of Ghana and her people in my own healing (and re-search) process. Most profoundly, as I've traveled to Ghana over the years, I can better see that when one uncovers the wisdom and lessons of their ancestors and is able to make deep and personal connections with the "earth of their birth," the lessons can be transformative. Grounded in such knowledge, one can walk, teach, and be in peace with self and others in more spiritual and ultimately more human ways.

Because the purpose of my journey here on earth is to teach, and because I believe "guides" and opportunities for uncovering one's purpose are often found in educational pursuits, I built the preschool in Mpeasem, Ghana, that was discussed earlier in this book. This was the beginning of work that continues to build bridges across continents, people, and traditions, to put it all back together in my life as an African American woman. However, even building the preschool, I was still within the familiar as an educator; I was still in the comfort of schools and schooling, in many ways similar to what I already know.

Coming full circle. I began to dream about the concept, about what it meant to live a life that really embraced the idea that everything was preparation for the next thing, that every mistake, challenge, joy, and life experience was preparation for what would come next. Mostly, I thought about coming full circle in terms that resonate with the academic life of research, teaching, and service that I have so enjoyed. But at some level, as I look at my résumé and reflect on my academic life, I have spent most of my time trying to change the academy, to create a fit between it and my understandings and realities as an African American woman. And throughout my career, I have seen this as a common pursuit among many colleagues of color. Whether in publication, in classes that we teach, in the everyday work in the academy, like many African ascendants, my academic life has focused on channeling my energies toward creating spaces and places and ways for people of color and others of conscience to create an academic life that resonates with spirit, with the intimate and personal understandings of how the world works (or doesn't) for African American women. These are the strivings highlighted in this book. In Chapter 1, the discussion focused on the way that epistemology for African American women embodies a distinguishably different culturally standpoint when centered in African and Black women's understandings of reality. In Chapter 2, I shared the paradox and possibilities of thinking about worldviews and their principles in paradigms when spirit and Black womanhood are brought to bear. The tensions, struggles, and joys of truly honoring our core beliefs about equity of access to education and its purposes with/in the world was the focus of Chapter 3. Chapter 4 embodied the notion of full circle in characterizing life and death as part of the same research moment in our academic lives, and how, when faced with such challenges, we might consider, in our academic lives, very different purposes with a very different criteria for measuring our success. In Chapter 5, I envisioned a different set of principles that might undergird our research methods when we surrender the importance of method to instead focus on the nature of the relationship that is called for between the researcher and the researched, contingent and different in every research situation. In my work in Ghana and here in the United States, I continue to see love, compassion, reciprocity, and ritual as important to an African centered ethic of research—and frankly, to all research endeavors. Chapter 6 encourages us to think deeply about boundaries of our training as researchers and teachers and to the sorts of transformations that are possible when we invite spirit to be central and present in our lives and work, especially in a profession that is so focused on words. This chapter also suggests that, from an African worldview, part of one's academic life must also focus on inviting new scholars and teachers into the spaces where we live and work. We are also encouraged to invite our students to create an academic life focused on teaching, research, and service in ways that embrace what Bell (2002) refers to as ethical ambition. Finally, as an African ascendant, I am challenged to think about Du Bois's notion of double consciousness in my work in Ghana in Chapter 7. Thus, this book has, as the level of thought and representation, been all about how one's epistemology, paradigm, research methods, teaching and ways of being necessarily change as we center our understandings in a spiritually and culturally grounded space.

And the more I've thought about how my work in Ghana, as an African ascendant has brought me full circle, the more I have been able to dream, to imagine a life that included being a scholar, teacher, and human being who sees "service [as] the rent you pay for living" (p. 6), as Edelman (1992) has suggested. I have dreamed of being part of a community of love and resistance that is focused on spiritual awareness and contemplation and peace as the path. I have dreamed about how my experiences in Ghana have brought me close to the earth, to embracing my natural surroundings as the spiritual teachers that they are. Mostly, I have found myself dreaming about an academic life that could include a consciousness of spirituality and African culture and thought without the boundaries and rules (spoken and unspoken) that have traditionally guided what we do, who we are, and the contexts of work as "professors." I have dreamed about the sort of academic life that really tried to respond to the purposes focused on early in this book and too often wondered whether it was even possible (given the slow wheels of change in most university contexts) to create a sort of academic life that really promotes life, that protects the most vulnerable among us, that really heals myself and others, and that really promotes and provides love.

I find myself moved and very excited by these dreams. But living a conscious academic life requires that each one of us live beyond dreams, with the sort of urgency that recognizes that our time on earth is limited but imbued with a particular purpose. And as Audre Lorde (1980) says:

> Living a self-conscious life . . . leaves a mark upon all of my life's decisions and actions . . . This consciousness gives my life another breath. It helps shape the words that I speak, the ways that I love, my politic of action, the strength of my vision and purpose, the depth of my appreciation for living. (p. 16)

And hers was not the only voice that I started to hear: It was as if the more I began to allow myself to talk of these dreams and to work toward a conscious, spirit-centered academic life, the more the Universe seemed to respond, opening doors for me to begin to reframe and transform this academic life of mine. And the voices became louder. There was Gandhi's voice, coming to me from a greeting card at the grocery store: "Be the change you wish in the world." There was my inspiration, Nelson Mandela: " Our deepest fear is not that we are inadequate. Our deepest fear is that we are powerful beyond measure."

With all these voices informing me, I began to explore the healing arts, to practice yoga, in addition to my daily writing meditations. I got married and went through a difficult divorce within the span of 14 months (that is, before marrying my dream partner, my Henry). And on the heels of that very difficult whirlwind, I went to a Yoga

Retreat for Women of Color, at Kripalu Yoga and Retreat Center in Lenox, Massachusetts. Developed by Maya Breuer, an African American yogini and teacher from Rhode Island, it was an amazing gathering of women from all over the country. The surroundings were absolutely stunning, located in the green and lush Berkshire Mountains. And it was here that my dreams became even more focused—and as suggested earlier, writing in my journal became a way to right things, a way to focus and make these dreams even clearer:

> I want to create communities of resistance that are at once beautiful, healing, refreshing both in surroundings and in substance surroundings. There should be people (Scholars? Healers? Teachers?) there all the time, sort of like a monastery or like Kripalu here, so that when people stay there, they feel some encouragement, some hope. Given our histories as Africans in the diaspora and our disconnections from the wisdom of the continent of Africa and her peoples (of which we are also a part), Africans need "homespaces" for rest and renewal that are grounded in our own cultural and historical understandings, images, and languages in order to become the global visionaries that we inherently are! I believe that as we work on healing projects that gather and refine and engage the African consciousness (just like Maya's doing here at Kripalu), we will ultimately enhance the human consciousness. And it will be called Full Circle Rest and Retreat Center. And it is my attempt to provide a space for myself and others to embrace education that is consciously spiritual, creative and purposeful. (Personal journal, 9/15/00)

And the more I wrote, the more the voices continued—and they affirmed the dream of the Full Circle work. There was a dear, very intuitive friend of mine: "This is an exquisite vision and it is your life's work . . . The transition from university will be a graceful one, not an abrupt one . . . There will be no problem that can't be overcome because this is *your* work." The task for me became one of embracing the faith and courage to take the bold steps needed to walk into this dream which might indeed move me further away from the known, from my academic life as a professor to one that lives even fuller versions of the ideas (and ideals) explored in this book.

"Are you running away from something or toward something?" This was my Dad's voice, asking the question that he'd taught us to use as a touchstone when we were unsure which direction to take, which decision to make. And Nelson Mandela's voice was again necessary encouragement, providing a sort of response to Dad's question: "You are a child of God. Your playing small doesn't serve the world." And frightened as I was, I knew that serving the world with the gifts I'd been given was indeed not only what I wanted to do more of: It was my purpose for being here. And I knew then that the work of Full Circle Retreats is what I need to be "running toward," that is, creating sites for education and learning as explicitly spiritual and healing practices, with Africa and her understandings as the context, the knowledge, and the foundation.

Some's (1997) words bear repeating here: Everything we engage in our lives is "primarily a practice ordered by spirit, or authorized by spirit and executed by someone who recognizes that [she] cannot, by herself, make happen what she has been invited towards" (p. viii). That whatever an academic life is, it is a life and work that is engaged on a continuum of life and death and life again, with particular power and meaning in our own lives and the lives of others. As humans, we have always been fascinated by the idea of a larger reality, of the idea of the "spirit." But what I've come to see in the experiences shared in this text is that it is in times of transition (whether perceived as positive or negative), we become aware that there can be so much more to an academic life than what we have historically undertaken or than we typically see. As an African American woman scholar, these transitions have been both big and small. They've happened in (finally) getting a paper published that you know will be provocative around issues of endarkened feminist thought. They've happened in the careful and thoughtful response of an African-ascendant colleague who provided the critical affirmation that one can delight in and learn from. They happened in becoming a Queen Mother in Ghana, and embracing the deep and rich history of the honor, the role and the work of helping to develop an entire village—and develop myself in the process. They've happened in the deaths of cherished loved ones. They've happened in relationships that call into question the very names you call yourself. Our transitions help us to comprehend the enormity of our lives and the multiplicity of dimensions on/in which they are being lived. Such transitions also are imbued with a sense of grace, because they often leave us confused, unknowing, and frightened, humbly aware of our hearts, minds, and spirits in relationship to the world and awakened to others in new and important ways.

And often, these transitions are inexplicable except in terms of something divine. And in an African sense, those of us who have recognized the role and outcomes of transitions in our academic lives also see that our understanding of ourselves becomes part of a larger reality: *I am because we are.* We can both see and experience our connections to others as the foundation of being human beings—and of being alive.

This book has been about transformation, the ways that an African American woman's academic life has changed as a consequence of consciously centering spirituality, African and Black feminist thought, and actual experiences in African contexts at the center of that life. But what does transformation really mean? How can we more consciously cultivate transformative life-changing experience for ourselves and others in our academic lives? What I am advocating here is that there can indeed be a transformative academic life. It is one that asks researchers and teachers to become what they are studying, to know as we are known (Palmer, 1983). And a transformative academic life asks us to subjectively engage ourselves—body, mind, *and* spirit—through direct experiences with the people, places, and phenomena we want to know more deeply. It becomes, as mentioned in Chapter 1, a way and a means to both serve humanity and to become more fully human in the process. I believe this happens not necessarily in a linear, but rather a more circular process, always turning back on itself, always reciprocal in nature. It is a creative life, as Feelings (1996) suggested at the start of this chapter, one that brings the spiritual notions of past, present, and future together for the benefit of wisdom and growth. But, most of all, a transformative academic life can and always is a political life, one that holds peace, justice, and love as its values and goals.

But to create such an academic life, we must also be open and prepared for life-changing transformations and see them as a normal part of our lives. They may not be something that we can plan for, but they are definitely something that will visit us at sometimes in our lives. And as African American women and Africans throughout the diaspora and on the continent, the horrors and trauma of the slave trade and the remnants that still manifest today in the worldwide condition of African people *demands* that we remember the healing and cultural legacies of Africa—and make conscious and continued connections with these legacies. However, those of us who experience transformative changes in our lives—and embrace them as spiritual openings for the lessons of our lives—seldom understand these transformations in their depth and complexity. Sometimes, we cannot even articulate their presence, let alone the impact they are having on our lives! Precipitated by a transition, a transformation means that something extraordinary comes forth, from places sometimes unknown to us. However, without our own openness to that shift, idea, or imagining, the whole experience may be so frightening that to step toward it is unthinkable. But it is exactly at that moment of fear that we must heed the voice of spirit: If it is urging us forward, we are the only impediment to our own becoming.

The process of transforming an academic life is as different as there are different people engaging in it. It happens in different stages, is precipitated by different events, and differs from one person to another. Within these pages, I have described the transformations that are happening in my academic life. I am sure there are places here that have resonated with you, depending on who you are, your particular perspectives, beliefs and values, and your spirit. I am sure there are other places that have not. I have come to see that spiritual strivings are simply the way we engage the transitions of our lives, academic and beyond, with spirit as our guide. I have also come to see that such strivings can be the path needed for becoming activist teachers and researchers who are spiritually grounded human beings and who do not see a separation between a spiritually engaged academic life and the hard work of ending oppression of self and others. And I've learned that discipline and prayer, when coupled with engaged study and research can indeed help one to see the world more clearly—and to intuitively know what to do and how to respond regardless of the context of one's work or one's vocation.

And that brings us full circle to the very purpose of teaching, research, and service when spirit and African cultural knowledge and experience are at the center. For me, I've realize that if my purpose is to help others to experience the healing wisdom of Africa, Black feminist praxis, and spirituality, the academic life that I've known will not be the academic life that I am moving toward. In fact, my conscious embrace of spirit in my work as an African American feminist and critical multicultural educator that may be slowly (but gracefully) moving me away from an academic life in university contexts and toward the overwhelming joy and vision of alternative contexts that bridge both the continent of Africa and her diaspora. And this transformation is bringing what a friend calls a "living sense of the alternative": The more I live and engage it, the more I know that coming full circle is the only work for us all to do.

Notes

1. I use the term "patterns of epistemology" to suggest that epistemology (how we know reality) is not a monolithic body, but is instead the ways that reality is a deeply cultured knowing that arises from and embodies the habits, wisdom, and patterns of its contexts of origin.

2. In the spirit of the epistemic nature and power of language discussed by Asante (1988), Kohain Hahlevi, a Hebrew Israelite rabbi uses the term "African-ascendant" to describe people of African heritage. In contrast to the commonly used term "descendent," he argues that African ascendant more accurately describes the upward and forward moving nature of African people throughout the diaspora as well as on the African continent herself. I subscribe to this notion.

3. With early roots in the work of Barbara Smith, Akasha Hull, Audrey Lorde, and more recently, Patricia Bell-Scott, Katie Cannon, Joy James, Ruth Farmer, Barbara Omolade, and Patricia Hill Collins, Black feminist voices argue that the very presence and positionality of Black women scholars and researchers gives us a coherent and distinctive cultural, analytical, and ideological location from which a coherent epistemology—and a different metaphor for educational research—can be articulated.

4. Many thanks to Dr. Dafina Martin, who wrote this prose piece during her graduate courses and work with me at Ohio State University.

5. This essay was presented as part of a symposium by the same name at the 1995 American Educational Research Annual Meeting. Many thanks to Pearl Cleage whose essay *Good brother blues* inspired the form of these life notes: The power and poetry of her language best captures both the frustration and the joy of my working life as an African American woman in the predominately white male world of the academy.

119

6. One of my current struggles, given the instrumentality of language suggested here is with the term "theory." From the Greek *theoros*, meaning spectator, it suggests explanations at a distance, with the researcher's positionality not accounted for as an integral part of the contours of the construction of reality. While I recognized the contradiction in using the term from an endarkened feminist epistemological space, I am currently searching for a more integrative and honest term to use in its place.

7. Given this discussion, the reader may assume that I am making an essentialist move here, a move arguing that self-definition is only a "Black [woman's] thang." And indeed, as a self-identified African American woman researcher, I choose to study African American women and communities and to be informed by African-centered theories and experiences. However, my stance relative to self-definition and responsibility is that, regardless of the race, gender, or other identity positions claimed by educational researchers, we all define our Selves as either insiders or outsiders (or some combination thereof) in the communities that we study. Thus, while there should be no doubt that an endarkened feminist epistemological standpoint *arises from* the voices and experiences of African American women, it is offered here as an alternative framework in the research community, useful to anyone who has the courage and desire to understand and embrace the metaphor of research as responsibility (in my/this case, to the African and African American communities and realities that I study) and who seeks to be informed and challenged by their research practices.

8. Both standpoint theory and the meanings (and even existence!) of concrete experiences in postmodern times may be problematic for some readers. While I do see involvement with the postmodern theoretical discussion as a way to draw attention to and examine the manner in which African American women's lives re-search themselves and are re-searched, I agree with Lubiano's (1991) notion that an African American feminist postmodernism "insists on the representation of history in the present moment" (p. 157), and "[needs] to be politically nuanced in a radical way, focus[ing] on such differences' implications especially in moments of oppositional transgressions" (p. 160). She goes on to suggest that "one of the things that an African American presence in postmodernism generally can offer [is a] constantly reinvigorated critique" (p. 153). My modest critique is my conscious choice to engage alternative cultural discourses other than postmodern discourse, in keeping with the spirit of an African ethos and frame of reference.

9. It is important to note that it was under the editorship of Jim Scheurich at QSE that *The substance of things hoped for, the evidence of things not seen: Examining an endarkened feminist epistemology in educational research and leadership* was finally published in 2000.

10. *Building a school* is one of a series of meditations from yet unpublished manuscript titled *Living Africa: A book of meditations*.

11. Mpeasem is particularly symbolic in the history of African people and the slave trade. According to Graham (1994), Kwodwo Brempoing bought a large number of slaves, but sent many far away to the bush that became Mpeasem, which translates in English to "I don't want no trouble." When the Europeans returned to load their vessels with human cargo, Brempong would show them fake graves of slaves who'd died since he'd replenished the last stock of slaves. They believed him and accepted the "survivors." This went on for a long time until he was able to people several villages. Mpeasem was one of them.

12. Thich Nhat Hanh, Buddhist teacher and monk wrote a poem entitled *Call me by my true names* (1998, pp. 174–176), which explores the ways in which each of us is one with all beings, from the man who is dying in a forced labor camp to a mayfly metamorphosing to a member of the politburo or an arms merchant. No one is really separate from any one. Hanh suggests, "I see all of them in me, and I see myself in all of them" (p. 174). This section of the book is dedicated to him and to this ideal.

13. *Becoming a Queen Mother* is part of a collection of meditations from my yet published manuscript titled *Living Africa: A book of meditations*.

14. Kaba is a style of dress worn by Ghanaian women, made from batik wax print cloth. It consists of a fitted top, often embellished with very elaborate necklines and sleeves, a form-fitting skirt with a slit, and a head wrap.

15. Nkosua Ohemaa means Queen Mother of Development in the Akan language of Twi.

16. "Who feels it knows it all" is a line of a song, taken from a Bob Marley tune of the same name. It is used often in television commercials in Ghana.

17. "Black American" is the term commonly used in Ghana to refer to people of African ascent who grew up in the United States.

18. Every slave dungeon along the West Coast of Africa has such a door. It is constructed in such a way that it was too small for any shackled African to have escaped, given that slaves were bound to one another and unable to move freely.

Bibliography

Anderson, M. L. (1993). Studying across difference: Race, class, and gender in qualitative research. In J. H. Stanfield (Ed.), *Race and ethnicity in research methods* (pp. 39–52). Newbury Park, CA: Sage Publications.

Ani, M. (1994). *Yurugu: An African-centered critique of European cultural thought and behavior.* Trenton, NJ: African World Press.

Appiah, K. A. (1992). *In my father's house: Africa in the philosophy of culture.* New York: Oxford University Press.

Armah, A. K. (1973). *Two thousand seasons.* Chicago: Third World Press.

Asante, M. K. (1988). *Afrocentricity.* Trenton, NJ: Africa World Press.

Baldwin, J. (1988). A talk to teachers. In R. Simonson & S. Walker (Eds.), *Multicultural literacy: Opening the American mind.* St. Paul: Graywolf.

Bell, D. (2002). *Ethical ambition: Living a life of meaning and worth.* New York: Bloomsbury.

Bell, D. (1992). *Faces at the bottom of the well: The permanence of racism.* New York: Basic Books.

Bell-Scott, P. (1994). *Life notes: Personal writings by contemporary Black women.* New York: W. W. Norton & Company.

Bethel, L. (1982). "This infinity of conscious pain": Zora Neale Hurston and the Black female literary tradition. In G. T. Hull, P. B. Scott, & B. Smith (Eds.), *All the women are white, all the Blacks are men, but some of us are brave* (pp. 176–188). New York: The Feminist Press.

Brown, E. B. (1988). African-American women's quilting: A framework for conceptualizing and teaching African-American women's history. In

M. R. Malson, E. Mudimbe-Boyi, J. F. O'Barr, & M. Wyer (Eds.), *Black women in America: Social science perspectives.* Chicago: The University of Chicago Press.

Cameron, J. (1999). *Transitions: Prayers and declarations for a changing life.* New York: Tarcher Putnam.

Cameron, J. (1997). *Heart steps: Prayers and declarations for a creative life.* New York: Tarcher Putnam.

Capper, C. A. (2003). Life lessons and a loving epistemology: A response to Julie Laible's loving epistemology. In M. D. Young & L. Skrla (Eds.), *Reconsidering feminist research in educational leadership.* Albany: SUNY.

Casey, K. (1995). The new narrative research in education. *Review of Research in Education,* 21, 211–253.

Cleage, P. (1990). *Mad at Miles.* New York: Ballantine.

Cobb, N. (2000). *In lieu of flowers: A conversation for the living.* New York: Pantheon.

Collins, P. H. (1998). *Fighting words: Black women and the search for justice.* Minneapolis: University of Minnesota Press.

Collins, P. H. (1990). *Black feminist thought: Knowledge, consciousness, and the politics of empowerment.* New York: Routledge.

Critchlow, W. (1995). Presentation given at The Ohio State University College of Education Annual Research Retreat, Columbus, OH, April 16, 1995.

Dillard, C. B. (2003). Cut to heal, not to bleed: A response to Handel Wright's "An endarkened feminist epistemology?" Identity, difference and the politics of representation in educational research, *International Journal of Qualitative Studies in Education,* 16, 227–232.

Dillard, C. B., Tyson, C. A., & Abdur-Rashid, D. (2000). My soul is a witness: Affirming pedagogies of the spirit. *International Journal of Qualitative Studies in Education,* 13, 447–462.

Dillard, C. B. (2000). The substance of things hoped for, the evidence of things not seen: Examining an endarkened feminist epistemology in educational research and leadership. *The International Journal of Qualitative Studies in Education,* 13, 661–681.

Dillard, C. B. (1995). Leading with her life: An African American feminist (re)interpretation of leadership for an urban high school principal. *Educational Administration Quarterly,* 31, 539–563.

Donmoyer, R. (1999). Paradigm talk revisited: How else might we character-ize the proliferation of research perspectives within our field? Unpub-lished proposal.

Du Bois, W. E. B. (1989). *The souls of Black Folk*. New York: Bantam.

Du Bois, W. E. B. (1986). *Dusk of dawn*. New York: Library of America.

Edelman, M. W. (1992). *The measure of our success: A letter to my children and yours*. Boston: Beacon.

Eisner, E. (1979). *The educational imagination: On the design and evaluation of school programs*. New York: Macmillan.

Ellison, R. (1952). *Invisible man*. New York: Vintage.

Ephirim-Dunker, A. (1997). *African spirituality: On becoming ancestors*. Tren-ton, NJ: Africa World Press.

Fine, M. (1992). *Disruptive voices: The possibilities of feminist research*. Ann Arbor, MI: University of Michigan Press.

Foster, M. (1990). The politics of race: Through the eyes of African Ameri-can teachers. *Journal of Education, 172*, 123–141.

Foundation for Inner Peace (1975). *A course in miracles*. New York: Penguin.

Freire, A. & Macedo, D. (Eds.) (2000). *The Paulo Freire reader*. New York: Continuum.

Freire, P. (1970). *Pedagogy of the oppressed*. New York: Continuum.

Gibran, K. (1998). *The prophet*. New York: Alfred A. Knopf.

Gitlan, A. (1994). The shifting terrain of methodological debates. In A. Gitlan (Ed.), *Power and method: Political activism and educational research* (pp. 1–12). New York: Routledge.

Golden, M., & Shreve, S. R. (Eds.) (1995). *Skin deep: Black women and white women write about race*. New York: Doubleday.

Gordon, B. (1990). The necessity of African American epistemology for educational theory and practice. *Journal of Education, 172*, 88–106.

Graham, E. (1994). *Cape Coast in history*. Cape Coast, Ghana: Anglican Printing Press.

Greene, M. (1988). *The dialectic of freedom* (pp. 1–23). New York: Teachers College Press.

Greene, M. (1978). *Landscapes of learning* (pp. 168–184). New York: Teachers College Press.

Guba, E. G., & Lincoln, Y. S. (1994). Competing paradigms in qualitative research. In N. K. Denzin & Y. S. Lincoln (Eds.), *The Handbook of Qualitative Research* (pp. 105–117). Thousand Oaks, CA: Sage.

Hanh, T. N. (1998). *Teachings on love.* Berkeley, CA: Parallex.

Hanh, T. N. & Berrigan, D. (2001). *The raft is not the shore: Conversations toward a Buddhist-Christian awareness.* Maryknoll, NY: Orbis Books.

Haraway, D. (1988). Situated knowledge: The science question in feminism and privilege of partial perspective. *Feminist Studies, 14,* 3 575–599.

Harding, S. (1987). *Feminism and methodology: Social science issues.* Bloomington: Indiana University Press.

Harris, A. (1990). Race and essentialism in feminist legal theory. *Stanford Law Review, 42,* 581–616.

hooks, b. (2001). Forward to *The raft is not the shore: Conversations toward a Buddhist-Christian awareness* (p. vii). Maryknoll, NY: Orbis Books.

hooks, b. (2000). *All about love: New visions.* NYC: William Morrow and Company.

hooks, b. (1995). Feminism in Black and White. In M. Golden & S. R. Shreve (Eds.), *Skin deep: Black women and white women write about race.* New York: Doubleday.

hooks, b. (1994). *Teaching to transgress: Education as the practice of freedom.* NY: Routledge.

hooks, b. (1989). *Talking back: Thinking feminist, thinking black.* Boston: South End Press.

Hull, A. G. (2001). *Soul talk: The new spirituality of African American women.* Rochester, VT: Inner Traditions.

Hull, G. T., Bell-Scott, P., & Smith, B. (1982). *All the women are white, all the blacks are men, but some of us are brave.* New York: The Feminist Press.

Hurston, Z. N. (1978). *Their eyes were watching God.* Urbana: University of Illinois.

James, J., & Farmer, R. (Eds.) (1993). *Spirit, space, and survival: African American women in (White) academe.* New York: Routledge.

James, J. (1993). African philosophy, theory, and "living thinkers." In J. James & R. Farmer (Eds). *Spirit, space and survival: Black women in (white) academe*. NY: Routledge.

James, S. M., & Busia, A. P. A. (Eds.) (1993). *Theorizing Black feminisms: The visionary pragmatism of Black women*. New York: Routledge.

Jeffries, R. (1997). The image of women in African cave art. *Journal of African Civilization*, 6, (1), 103–104.

King, D. K. (1988). Multiple jeopardy, multiple consciousness: The context of a Black feminist ideology. *Signs*, 14, 4–72.

King, Jr., M. L. (1967). *Where do we go from here: Chaos or community?* New York: Bantam.

Ladd, F. (1996). *Sarah's psalm*. New York: Simon & Schuster.

Ladson Billings, G. (1994). *The dreamkeepers: Successful teachers of African American children*. San Francisco: Jossey-Bass.

Lather, P. (1986). Issues of validity in openly ideological research: Between a rock and a soft place. *Interchange*, 17, 63–84.

Lightfoot, S. L. (1994). *I've known rivers: Lives of loss and liberation*. Reading, MA: Addison-Wesley.

Lorde, A. (1984). *Sister outsider*. Freedom, CA: The Crossing Press.

Lorde, A. (1980). *The cancer journals*. San Francisco: Spinsters/Aunt Lute.

Lubiano, W. (1991). Shuckin' off the African-American native other: What's "po-mo" got to do with it? *Cultural Critique*, 18, 149–186.

McCarthy, C., & Critchlow, W. (Eds.) (1993). *Race and representation in education*. New York: Routledge.

Morrison, T. (1993). *Playing in the dark: Whiteness and the literary imagination*. New York: Vintage.

Morrison, T. (1987). *Beloved*. New York: Alfred A. Knopf.

Omi, M., & Winant, H. (1993). On the theoretical concept of race. In C. McCarthy & W. Critchlow (Eds.), *Race and representation in education* (pp. 3–10). New York: Routledge.

Omi, M., & Winant, H. (1986). *Racial formation in the United States: From the 1960s to the 1990s*. NY: Routledge.

Omolade, B. (1994). *The rising song of African American women*. New York: Routledge.

Packwood, A., & Sikes, P. (1996). Adopting a postmodern approach to research. *Qualitative Studies in Education, 9,* 335–345.

Palmer, P. (1983). *To know as we are known: Education as a spiritual journey.* San Francisco: Harper.

Paris, P. J. (1995). *The spirituality of African people: Toward a common moral discourse.* Minneapolis: Augsburg Fortress Press.

Peck, M. S. (1978). *The road less travelled: A new psychology of love, traditional values and spiritual growth.* New York: Touchtone.

Richards, D. M. (1980). *Let the circle be unbroken: The implications of African spirituality in the diaspora.* Lawrenceville, NJ: The Red Sea Press.

Richardson, L. (1994). Writing: A method of inquiry. In N. K. Denzin & Y. S. Lincoln (Eds.), *The Handbook of Qualitative Research* (pp. 516–529). Thousand Oaks: Sage.

Rilke, R. M. (1934). *Letters of a young poet.* New York: W. W. Norton & Company.

Rubin, H. (1999). *Soloing: Realizing your life's ambition.* New York: Harper.

Scheurich, J., & Young, M. (1997). Coloring epistemologies: Are our research epistemologies racially biased? *Educational Researcher, 26,* 4–16.

Smith, D. (1994). *The Tao of dying.* Stanton Park, DC: Caring Publishing.

Smith, D. E. (1987). *The everyday world as problematic: A feminist sociology.* Boston: Northeastern University Press.

Some, M. P. (1994). *Of water and the spirit: Ritual, magic, and initiation in the life of an African shaman.* New York: G. P. Putnam's Sons.

Stanfield, J. H. (1994). Ethnic modeling in qualitative research. In N. Denzin & Y. Lincoln (Eds.), *Handbook of qualitative research* (pp. 175–188). NY: Sage.

Stanfield, J. H. (1993). Epistemological considerations. In J. H. Stanfield, (Ed.), *Race and ethnicity in research methods* (pp. 16–38). Newbury Park, CA: Sage Publications.

Stepanik, M. (2001). *Journey through heartsongs.* Alexandria, VA: VSP Books.

Terry, R. (1996). *Kwanzaa: The seven principles.* White Plains, NY: Peter Pauper.

Thiongo, N. W. (1986). *Decolonising the mind: The politics of language in African literature.* Portsmouth, NH: Heinemann.

Tierney, W. G. (1994). On method and hope. In A. Gitlan (Ed.), *Power and method: Political activism and educational research* (pp. 97–115). New York: Routledge.

Tyson, C. A. (1998). A response to "Coloring epistemologies: Are our qualitative research epistemologies racially biased?" *Educational Researcher*, 27, 21–22.

Vanzant, I. (1996). *The spirit of a man*. New York: HarperCollins Publishers.

Wade-Gayles, G. (Ed.) (1995). *My soul is a witness: African American women's spirituality*. Boston: Beacon Press.

Walker, A. (1996). *The same river twice: Honoring the difficult*. New York: Scribner.

Webster's Desk Dictionary (2001). New York: Random House.

West, C. (1993). *Race matters*. Boston: Beacon Press.

Woodson, C. G. (1990). *The mis-education of the Negro*. Trenton, NJ: Africa World Press.

Wright, H. (2003). "An endarkened feminist epistemology?" Identity, difference and the politics of representation in educational research. *International Journal of Qualitative Studies in Education*, 16, (2), 197–214.

Wright, R. (1945). *Black boy*. New York: Harper & Row.

Wynter, S. (1992). *Do not call us Negros: How multicultural textbooks perpetuate racism*. San Francisco: Aspire Books.

Yenne-Donmoyer, J. & Donmoyer, R. (April 1994). In their own words: A readers theatre presentation of middle school students writing about writing. Script presented at the Annual Meeting of the American Educational Research Association, New Orleans, LA.

Young, E. (1992). *Seven blind mice*. San Francisco: Philomel.

Index